This book is dedicated to
Slick Bryant and Frank Wedertz
Mono County, California historians
who shared much of their
great knowledge with me.
Rest in Eternal Peace
with our Lord, Jesus Christ.

Table of Contents

Author's Introduction 5

Chapter One 9
Sam Clemens Becomes A Silver Miner

Chapter Two 17
Aurora, Nevada

Chapter Three 31
Sam Goes to Aurora

Chapter Four 43
Aurora Takes Hold of Sam and his Money

Chapter Five 49
The Annipolitan and the Wide West Mine

Chapter Six 55
Sam and the Lost Cement Gold Mine

Chapter Seven 65
Sam Explores Mono Lake and Vicinity

Chapter Eight 85
Sam Clemens Leaves Aurora

Chronology 90

Acknowledgements 92

Bibliography 92

Index 94

AUTHOR'S INTRODUCTION

This is the first in a series of five books I have written about Mark Twain's life in the West.

MARK TWAIN: HIS ADVENTURES AT AURORA AND MONO LAKE, tells of Sam Clemens' arrival in Nevada Territory in 1861 and concentrates on his silver mining experiences at Aurora, Nevada, north of Mono Lake. This book, like others in the series, is written so it may be read and understood independently of other books in the series.

At Aurora, Nevada, Sam Clemens spent nearly six months as a silver miner trying to strike it rich. He nearly succeeded; fortunately for American literature, he did not. For failure as a silver miner at Aurora caused Clemens to turn to writing as a serious career.

Though most Americans associate Mark Twain with *Tom Sawyer* and the Mississippi River, Sam Clemens spent six very important years in Nevada and California. His mining experiences at Aurora led to his first full time reporting job on the *Territorial Enterprise* at Virginia City near Reno where Clemens adopted his pen name, Mark Twain.

Mark Twain was in spirit a Westerner. "Mark Twain" was born in the West and there his early writing career was nurtured. Some of his best and funniest writing is in *Roughing It*, his second book, which tells of his many humorous adventures in the West.

The goal of this book is to make modern readers aware of Mark Twain's Western years and how they influenced his career as an important American writer and personality.

In writing this book, I have endeavored to rely on what I consider primary sources. These are the letters Mark Twain wrote to relatives and friends, the journals and recollections of men who knew Mark Twain in the West and early Western newspaper reports.

Secondary sources are Twain's published writings, primarily, *Roughing It*, and *The Autobiography of Mark Twain*, which are at times unreliable due to Twain's wonderful imagination and his need to exaggerate.

Other books in this series which cover specific periods of Mark Twain's Western career are: *MARK TWAIN: His Life In Virginia City, Nevada, MARK TWAIN: Jackass Hill and the Jumping Frog, On The Road With Mark Twain In California and Nevada* and *Mark Twain In San Francisco*. Readers may use the order form at the end of this book to order autographed copies by mail.

... remember the Lord thy God: for it is he that giveth thee power to get wealth ...

Deuteronomy 8:18

"I've been a prospector and know pay rock from poor when I find it — just with a touch of the tongue ... And I've been a silver miner and know how to dig and drill, and put in a blast."

Mark Twain, 1890

Sam Clemens at the age of twenty-seven not long after he had left Aurora. Photograph was taken in San Francisco in 1863. *Mark Twain Project, University of California, Berkeley.*

CHAPTER ONE

Sam Clemens Becomes A Silver Miner

In the pine nut hills 20 miles north of Mono Lake, east of the Sierra Nevada and not far from Yosemite National Park, are the remains of Aurora, Nevada, once a great silver mining town and briefly the home of Sam Clemens, shortly before he adopted his pen name, Mark Twain. There is little left to mark this historical place where thousands once lived and a great American author began his writing career. The sturdy brick buildings built in great faith when Aurora boomed in the early 1860's, were torn down after World War II. For nearly ninety years they had stood in this desolate region, and for more than forty years they had stood vacant, the cold wind blowing through their broken windows and the snow crushing their weary roofs. Then an industrious American saw the value of Aurora's lonesome brick buildings. The great historic buildings were torn down brick by brick and sold, becoming parts of walls of unknown buildings far from here. Today, all that remains are dirt roads, great holes in the hillsides, foundations, a few shacks and the cemetery which is in fairly good condition. Here among squat pine nut trees, buried beneath white marble and granite stones, are many adventurous men who believed as Sam Clemens once believed, that the Aurora silver mines would make them rich.

Aurora lay in a squat, high mountain valley at 8,000 feet surrounded by hills dotted with emerald green pine nut trees. The mining district was named Esmeralda, Spanish for emerald. The hills today bear the scars of men who dug into their sides searching for gold and silver. No one works the mines these days, but in the early 1860's many men struggled, fought and died to own these forgotten holes in the ground. One of these men was young Sam Clemens.

Sam Clemens arrived in Carson City, Nevada Territory, August 14, 1861. He had tagged along with his older brother Orion, who had been appointed Secretary of Nevada Territory. Nevada Territory had become important to the Government because of the discovery of huge deposits of gold and silver at Gold Hill and Virginia City, 15 miles northeast of Carson City. The Federal Government needed gold and silver to finance the Union's efforts against the Confederacy.

Though a Southerner by birth having been born at Florida, Missouri in 1835, Sam Clemens did not want to fight in the Civil War and he was not motivated by politics. The Civil War had interfered with his life drastically. Until the Civil War broke out, Clemens was content as a highly paid river boat pilot on the Mississippi. But the war had closed traffic along the river and Clemens had lost his high paying job.

Out of a job, afraid he might be forced to pilot military gunboats and eager to make his fortune, Sam Clemens saw Orion's timely appointment as an escape from a troublesome situation and a possible means of getting rich in the West. Sam and Orion pledged to unite their energies toward one common goal: to win their fortunes. July 26, the brothers left St. Joseph, Missouri by Overland stage for Carson City.

Arriving in Carson City, Sam first worked as Orion's private secretary. Learning his salary was deducted from Orion's meager salary, Sam decided to try something else.

He made several trips to Lake Tahoe, then called Lake Bigler. He fell in love with the lake and claimed 300 acres of timber. But when his "house" burned down, a sort of shrub hut which held his timber claim, Clemens gave up timber "ranching" and headed back to Carson City.

A year earlier, the discovery of huge deposits of gold and silver at Gold Hill and Virginia City had attracted thousands of men to northwestern Nevada Territory. Mining parties scoured desolate regions of the Territory searching for the next bonanza. Exaggerated accounts of fantastic strikes drove men out into the mountains and deserts often on wild goose chases. Prospectors had a weakness for believing that there was a pot of gold just over the next hill or at the next camp.

In the fall of 1861, one of the most talked about mining camps was Aurora, sometimes referred to as Esmeralda. With all the talk of its rich mines, Clemens became curious. In October, Clemens made a

Orion Clemens, Sam's older brother, who was appointed Secretary of Nevada Territory in 1861. *Nevada Historical Society.*

horseback trip 130 miles southeast of Carson City to Aurora to investigate the silver mines. There an acquaintance gave him 50 feet in the Black Warrior claim. Clemens, unprepared for a long winter stay, returned to Carson City planning to go back to Aurora shortly.

But back in Carson City, Clemens was bombarded by news of a supposedly even more promising mining area, Unionville, Humboldt Mining District, 200 miles northeast of Carson City.

In December, Sam Clemens succumbed to a horrible case of silver fever. He became as mad as the rest. Clemens and three friends, Billy Claggett, Gus Oliver, both lawyers and Mr. Tillou (Mr. Ballou in *Roughing It*) a sixty year old blacksmith and veteran prospector, bought a decrepit wagon and loaded it with 180 pounds of provisions and headed for Humboldt Mining District. It didn't matter that it was the middle of winter and that the men had nothing to live in once they reached Humboldt. Clemens expected to find "masses of silver lying all about the ground glittering in the sun on the mountain summits."

Each man had his own horse, and two "miserable" horses sort of pulled the wagon. The trip took longer than they expected. Twain later wrote, "We could have accomplished the journey in ten days if we had towed the horses behind the wagon.." Prospecting parties they met along the way suggested they put the horses *in the wagon* but Mr. Tillou said they could not because the horses were "bituminous from long deprivation."

Twain explained Mr. Tillou's strange vocabulary in *Roughing It*:

... What Mr. Tillou customarily meant, when he used a long word, was a secret between himself and his Maker. He was one of the best and kindest hearted men that ever graced a humble sphere of life. He was gentleness and simplicity itself — and unselfishness, too. Although he was more than twice as old as the eldest of us, he never gave himself any airs, privileges, or exemptions on that account. He did a young man's share of the work and did his share of conversing and entertaining from the general stand-point of any age ... His one striking peculiarity was his Partingtonian fashion of loving and using big words for their own sakes, and independent of any bearing they might have upon the thought he was purposing to convey. He always let his ponderous syllables fall with an easy unconsciousness that left them wholly without offensiveness. In truth his air was so natural and so simple that one was always

80

Unionville

Reno

Virginia City

Gold Hill

Silver City

50

Dayton

Lake Tahoe

Carson City

NEVADA
CALIFORNIA

N

Yerington

Wellington

395

Aurora

Hawthorne

Bridgeport

Pole line Road

Bodie

To Yosemite

167

Lee Vining

Mono Lake

To Las Vegas

120

Mining Towns

June Lake

120

Highways

To Los Angeles

Dirt Rds

Mammoth Lakes

13

catching himself accepting his stately sentences as meaning something, when they really meant nothing in the world. If a word was long and grand and resonant, that was sufficient to win the old man's love, and he would drop that word into the most out-of-the-way place in a sentence or a subject, and be as pleased with it as if it were perfectly luminous with meaning.

Clemens had a special affection for Tillou who he referred to in his letters as "Dad," or "the old man." Tillou was a loveable, comical fellow who got himself into trouble without meaning to. After Clemens returned to Carson City, he wrote Billy Claggett at Unionville:

Keep an eye on the old man, Billy, and don't let him get too enthusiastic, because if he does, he will begin to feel young again like he did when he fell in the [Carson] river at Honey-Lake's; and being a lecherous old cuss anyhow, he might ravish one of the Pi-utes and bring on an Indian war ...

letter, February 28, 1862

In another letter, Clemens wrote Claggett he was trying to get a copy of *Fannie Hill* for the "old man."

Of their fifteen day trip to Unionville, Humboldt Mining District, Twain wrote:

It was a hard, wearing, toilsome journey, but it had its bright side; for after each day was done and our wolfish hunger appeased with a hot supper of fried bacon, bread, molasses and black coffee, the pipe-smoking, song singing and yarn-spinning around the evening campfire in the still solitudes of the desert was a happy, care-free sort of recreation that seemed the very summit and culmination of earthly luxury. It is a kind of life that has potent charm for all men, whether city or country-bred.

Roughing It

The party camped near the Humboldt Sink for two days and tried to drink the brackish water but it was like drinking lye. Mr. Tillou managed to concoct a form of coffee from the water but after drinking half a cup, threw the rest away saying it was, "too technical for him."

14

Finally, Sam and his friends reached Unionville in a terrible snowstorm. Unionville was a camp of eleven cabins and a flag pole. Six of the cabins were on one side of a deep canyon and five faced these on the other side. It was terribly cold and there was little firewood. The four men quickly threw up a crude shelter of rock and shrubs. In a letter to Billy Claggett written after Clemens had left Unionville, Clemens wrote, "Indeed, it is a great source of gratification to me to review my efforts up there in the gulch ... If I do possess one shining talent it is that of building willow houses out of rocks and dirt and things." He added a note about their fire-place, "I superintended that little piece of architecture ..."

Led by the experienced Tillou, Sam and his friends hiked up the steep hillsides above the town searching for gold and silver. Eventually they found an outcropping of quartz. Tillou explained that the gold and silver were sometimes found embedded in the quartz. The problem, he said, was that the ledge of quartz sometimes extended deep into the earth *for miles*. Their job was to sink a shaft and hopefully strike the ore bearing portion of the ledge.

The four made a written notice and posted their claim. They called their discovery the "Monarch of the Mountains" and filed the claim with the mining recorder's office. Then they went to work sinking a shaft.

After about a week of hard labor, Clemens figured there must be an easier way to make money. He, like others, discovered money could be made not in the toil of mining but in buying and trading "feet," or shares of mining claims. So Clemens and his partners went about buying and trading "feet" like the rest of the camp. Clemens and his partners became just as mad as the rest of Unionville's crazed population. But their visions of silver fortunes did not make them rich and they like the rest of the camp, could not pay the grocer. "It was the strangest phase of life one can imagine," Twain later wrote, "It was a beggars revel."

Like numbers of mining camps, Unionville was more talk than substance. After no more than two weeks, Clemens was fed up with the cold and the poor prospects of the camp. He left Unionville in early January with Mr. Tillou and another man and headed back for Carson City. By January 9, Orion believed Sam was stranded at Honey-Lake Smith's or at Ragtown, where a desert rainstorm had caused the Carson

River to swell to such a degree that it could not be crossed safely. Sam waited until the river subsided and continued his trip to Carson City, still not rich, but wiser for the wear and tear.

CHAPTER TWO

Aurora, Nevada

By mid-January, 1862, Clemens was back in Carson City and living with Orion. Though he had not struck it rich at Unionville, Clemens was not ready to give up his dream of making his fortune as a silver miner.

Only a few weeks after his return to Carson City, the silver mines of Aurora, Nevada were occupying his thoughts. In a letter to his mother February 8, he gave his reasons for leaving Unionville: "I came down here [to Carson City] from Humboldt, in order to look after our Esmeralda [Aurora] interests, and my sorebacked horse and the bad roads have prevented me from making the journey [to Aurora.]" What also may have kept him from going back to Aurora was the memory of his cold, miserable trip to Unionville.

Sam's "interests" at Aurora were his shares in the "Black Warrior" claim and the "Horatio and Derby" which Orion and he had purchased in the fall. Clemens was part owner in these claims with Orion, Horatio Phillips and Bob Howland, Governor Nye's nephew and future Aurora town marshal. By early February, Horatio Phillips had written Sam from Aurora that they had driven a 52 foot tunnel into the "Horatio and Derby." They hadn't struck ore worth mentioning but they had tapped several springs. Since water was scarce at Aurora, Sam and Horatio figured if nothing else they could sell the water.

Still learning about mining and prospecting, Clemens was naive concerning his Aurora mining claims. He believed his partners would strike the ore bearing ledge of the "Horatio and Derby" by June and that by July the mine would be paying handsomely. He expected to leave Nevada in July a rich man and visit his mother and sister in St. Louis. But in February, he was nearly broke and complained to his mother that he wished he had the money to buy more mining shares:

> Now there's the "Horatio," for instance. There are five or six shareholders in it, and I <u>know</u> I could buy half of their interests at, say $20 per foot, now that flour is worth $50 per barrel and they are pressed for money. But I am hard up myself, and can't buy — and in June they'll strike the ledge and then "good-bye canary." I can't get it for love or money. Twenty dollars a foot! Think of it. For ground that is <u>proven</u> to be rich.
>
> letter, February 8, 1862

Ever the optimist, Clemens was perturbed that he didn't have the money to buy what he considered a fortune maker. Clemens was still learning about silver mining. Naive, he was susceptible to every good deal that was flashed before his eyes. Once Clemens learned the silver mining game, he proved to be a fairly sensible and shrewd businessman. Clemens would overcome his mining naivete in a matter of months.

From the twenty-two letters Clemens wrote during this period, it's clear Sam and Orion were partners in all their mining dealings. Orion supplied Sam money to live on and to invest in various mining claims. But it is also clear, Sam, with a keener business sense, felt he was the boss. He insisted that Orion leave business matters to him and wrote his mother:

> But I am at the helm, now. I have convinced Orion that he hasn't business talent enough to carry on a peanut stand, and he has solemnly promised me that he will meddle no more with mining, or other matters not connected with the Secretary's office. So, you see, if mines are to be bought and sold, or tunnels run, or shafts sunk, parties have to come to me — and me only. I'm the "firm" you know.

Sam learned about Orion's business incompetence firsthand. He had worked for two of Orion's newspapers, one in Hannibal, Missouri, another at Keokuk, Iowa. Orion ran both papers into the ground. Orion was kind, thoroughly honest and good but he was no businessman and

18

↑ To Carson City

☆ AurorA

395

13 miles   BODIE

17 miles
Bodie CANYON

Pole Line Rd

HAWTHORNE →

☆ Castle PK.
Trumbol Lake

ConWAy Summit   MoNoville

167

Aurora To Owens River Road

Mill Creek

☆ Lundy   MoNo LAke Park

BLACK POINT

MONO LAKE

NegiT Is

PAAHA Is.

SierRA NevAda MoUNTAiNs

To YosemiTe

LEE ViNiNG

TuFA ReseRve   NAVy Beach

120

JuNe LAke

MoNo cRaters

MTNs.

BENTON

MAMMoTh LAKES

OWENs RiveR

Long Valley

BENTON Crossing

White MTNs

DirT Rds

Highways

Mining Towns ☆

↓ To Los Angeles

Crowley Lake

19

Sam knew it.

Shortly after arriving in Nevada Territory, seeking ways to earn money, Sam made a deal with the St. Louis *Gate City,* to write several travel letters about Nevada Territory. He wrote his first letter October 26, 1861. Travel letters were highly popular. Without radio and television, people relied on newspapers and magazines for news and entertainment. Letters by men who visited far away places — like Nevada Territory, were interesting and much in vogue.

Clemens had written travel letters for several newspapers and discovered he had a talent for it. At eighteen, he wrote letters for the Muscatine (Iowa) *Journal.* In 1856, he wrote a series of letters for the Keokuk (Iowa) *Daily Post.* In 1859 and 1861, he published humorous burlesque sketches in the New Orleans *Crescent.*

Sam had been involved with printing and newspapers since the age of thirteen. When his father died when Sam was twelve, Sam pleaded with his mother to permit him to leave school. Jane Clemens agreed. Sam became a printer's apprentice and helped print the local paper.

Several years later, Orion, a printer by trade, bought the Hannibal *Journal* and hired Sam as a printer and typesetter. When Orion left town, Sam took over as editor. During Orion's absences, Sam wrote and published humorous sketches about local characters. The locals appreciated Sam's humor but Orion scolded Sam for taking liberties. Sam promised never to do it again but as soon as Orion was gone, Sam was up to his old tricks.

After turning eighteen, Sam traveled around eastern America for several years. He visited New York, Philadelphia, Cincinnati, Washington, D.C. and Keokuk. In each city or town he found work as a printer or typesetter. During this period Clemens wrote for pleasure, experimenting with new styles. Later, when he was learning river piloting, Horace Bixby noticed that Sam was "always scribbling" when he wasn't piloting.

Now toward the end of January, 1862, Sam wrote his second travel letter for the *Gate City.* This, like his first, was a somewhat contrived letter from a son in Nevada Territory to his mother in St. Louis. Much of this second letter told about his trip to Humboldt. Clemens included humorous incidents. These letters are important because they are the basis for several chapters in *Roughing It.* That Clemens was practicing his writing craft in Nevada would prove helpful in landing his first full time writing job.

Sam was convinced that his and Orion's Aurora mining investments would pay off. January 31, he wrote Orion's wife, Mollie, that he believed their mining claims "will be paying handsomely" by July. He shared with Mollie his feelings about his future wealth and the woman he hoped to share it with:

I am not married yet, and I never will marry until I can afford to have servants enough to leave my wife in the position for which I designed her, viz: — as a companion. I don't want to sleep with a three-fold Being who is cook, chambermaid and washerwoman all in one. I don't mind sleeping with female servants as long as I am a bachelor — by no means — but after I marry, that sort will be "played out" you know.

This comment and others, provides insight into the kind of life Clemens wished to have. He would not marry until he could provide his wife with the kind of luxury he believed she desired. His wife was not to be a maid and a cook. He desired to have servants.

Clemens kept his promise. He did not marry until he was thirty-five when he had achieved financial success. He did have servants as he had planned.

At twenty-five, Clemens had tasted the good life as a river boat pilot where he had made an extravagant living. He was determined to become successful in the West. He wrote his sister, "I have been a slave several times in my life, but I'll never be one again." Clemens believed with blind faith, that his Aurora mining properties would make him rich. Ironically, failure as an Aurora silver mine would cause him to turn to writing as a means of earning his living. In a matter of five years, his writing — not his mining claims, would earn him national notoriety and the income he desired.

Sam stayed in Carson City through the early months of 1862 waiting for spring to return to the mountains. There would be no point in going to Aurora now. The camp was buried in snow; prospecting would be impossible. It was cold there, food and supplies were extravagant and there was little suitable shelter. Furthermore, the only way to get to Aurora was on horseback. The first stage service to Aurora would not be available until spring.

February 28, Sam wrote Billy Claggett at Unionville that he was "going to Esmeralda [Aurora] with Bunker in a week or ten days from now." Clemens may have made a trip to Aurora in March but it is doubtful for he was in Carson City, April 2 when he wrote a letter to his mother.

Clemens probably left for Aurora between April 2-10. He was in Aurora by April 13, when he wrote his first letter from Aurora to Orion.

Aurora, Nevada is located 130 miles southeast of Carson City and 23 miles southwest of Hawthorne, Nevada, the nearest town. The site is fairly accessible by highways and graded dirt roads.

If you are in Carson City, the quickest route to Aurora is to take Highway 395, 90 miles south of Bridgeport, California. Seven miles south of Bridgeport a road sign points the way to Bodie, once a famous gold mining town, today a ghost town and California State Park. I suggest you visit Bodie; it's on the way to Aurora. The fact is, there is more in Bodie than at Aurora and it will give you an idea what Aurora, the mining town, was like. The road to Bodie is paved for ten miles, the last three miles are not paved and fairly rough but trailers and RV's make it in just fine. For a helpful guide and history of Bodie, pick up a copy of *THE GUIDE TO BODIE AND EASTERN SIERRA HISTORIC SITES,* by the author at the Bodie Museum or at stores in Bridgeport. This book contains maps, road directions, information and photos of Aurora.

Aurora is 17 miles northeast of Bodie. After visiting Bodie, you must go north around the town and down Bodie Canyon for 13 miles. This is a dirt road and can be rough depending on whether or not the spring runoff has wrecked portions of the road. To be safe, ask the Bodie Park rangers about the condition of Bodie Canyon road before proceeding down the canyon. Thirteen miles down Bodie Canyon you will reach a sandy flats and a fork in the road. Turn right, go east, 4 miles to the Aurora site. The Aurora cemetery is about a half mile this side of Aurora. A sign should point to your right to the cemetery if someone hasn't stolen it or shot it down.

If you are approaching from Los Angeles or the Mammoth Lakes area, take Highway 395 north past Lee Vining to California Highway 167. This is known as Pole Line Road. Go east about 45 miles. About five miles this side of Hawthorne a well graded dirt road — Lucky Boy Grade, leads 25 miles southwest to Aurora.

There are no stores or gas stations at Bodie nor between Bodie and Aurora. If approaching Aurora via Lucky Boy Grade, there are no stores

Deserted Aurora saloons in the late 1920's. *Burton Frasher photo.*

23

or gas stations between the highway and Aurora. To avoid tragedy in this rough, desert country, carry plenty of water, at least one gallon per person per day. Fill up your gas tank and safely carry extra gas in an appropriate metal container. Fill your radiator with coolant and water. Bring extra water for the radiator. Of course bring food. Be sure to tell someone where you are going, show them the route you intend to take and tell them when you will be back. Don't do something stupid like getting lost in the desert or running out of gas — like I've been known to do. It's also wise to travel with someone else so you can help one another if your car breaks down. And take a shovel in case you plan to get stuck in the sand.

Gold was discovered at Aurora, August 25, 1860 by Jim Corey, Jim Braley and E.R. Hicks. Corey and Braley were from San Jose. They had met Hicks, part Cherokee, in Virginia City. The three prospectors were supposedly heading for Mono Lake, but more likely Monoville, a placer gold discovery just north of Mono Lake. Gold had been discovered at Monoville in 1859. Large numbers of men crossed the Sierra in the spring of 1860 and made their way to Monoville. The Aurora discovery was partly due to the excitement the Monoville gold discovery had caused.

Corey, Braley and Hicks were camped in the Aurora area, when Hicks searching for game and water, broke off pieces of a quartz outcropping and found gold. This became known as the Winnemucca Lode located near the west crest of Esmeralda Hill. That afternoon, Corey located three more lodes: the Esmeralda, the Cape and the Plata. Corey being well read, named their discovery site, Aurora, meaning "Goddess of Dawn." He called the mining district "Esmeralda," Spanish for emerald because of the beautiful pine nut trees which cover the hills.

Within two months of the discovery, prospectors had made 357 claims. Discoverers Corey and Braley sold their claims for $30,000 each — a huge sum at the time, and settled in Santa Clara, California. Hicks sold out for $10,000 and returned to Arkansas.

In April, 1861, the first stage arrived from Carson City in Aurora. The fare cost $20 and the trip took 24 hours. Like any out of the way place, everything at Aurora was expensive. Meals were 75 cents each, as much as $10 a week. Gull eggs from nearby Mono Lake were much appreciated and sold for 75 cents a dozen. The cost of feeding a horse a single day was $3.

When Sam Clemens arrived in Aurora in April, 1862, the camp

Bodie, California, the north part of town, in the early 1880's. Row of white buildings face on Main Street. The small shacks behind Main Street were located on Virginia Alley, also called Bonanza Street, the Redlight District. Here Rosa May and other girls worked until World War I. *Courtesy Frank Wedertz.*

consisted of 2,000 frenzied miners living in everything from holes in the hillsides, to crude stone shelters, tents and cabins. There were the usual array of saloons, whore houses, tent restaurants and general good stores. Many brick buildings were already being erected.

The *Esmeralda Star* began publishing May 17, 1862. By August, 1862, Aurora had swelled to 3,000 and the camp boasted 22 saloons.

By April, 1863, stages were bringing in 25-30 newcomers a day. Lots were selling for $2500-5,000 each. The camp now had a population of 4,000, 200 of which were women and a school was built for the 80 children. Aurora had 761 houses, 64 of them brick; 22 saloons, 2 churches, Masonic and Odd Fellows organizations and two newspapers. The population eventually peaked at between 6-10,000.

Early milling of ores was done by the arrastre method, first used by the Mexicans. In this primitive form of milling, horses or mules hitched to spokes on a large wheel walked in a continuous circle for hours dragging rocks over a circular pit of ore. Gradually the ore was ground down and the silver and gold were extracted. By June, 1861, the first amalgamating mill was built.

A total of sixteen mills were built with 200 stamps crushing ore. The largest mills were the Real Del Monte, built at a cost of $250,000 and the Antelope Mill. Both were huge brick structures in the Gothic style. The Real Del Monte had a battery of 30 stamps with 36 wheeler pans. The Antelope Mill had fewer stamps and pans. Both mills were powered by steam.

For a time there was a dispute as to whether Aurora was in California or Nevada. Both California and Nevada claimed the town. In the spring of 1861, the California legislature made Aurora, Mono County seat. But in October, 1863, a survey party settled the dispute: Aurora was four miles inside the Nevada border. Mono County officials grudgingly moved the county seat to Bodie, at that time a struggling mining camp. Aurora became Esmeralda county seat.

By 1865, Aurora's initial excitement had subsided. Surface bonanzas had produced 24 million dollars but much of the money was wasted by incompetent mining companies. Several things contributed to the camp's hard times. The original veins were shallow and exhausted at a depth of 94 feet. The mines and mining companies were largely mismanaged. Grossly expensive mills were often idle and did not successfully extract the gold and silver. Water in the mines was another problem. When hidden springs were tapped, pumps could not remove

The earliest known photograph of Aurora, Nevada, taken around 1865. Esmeralda Hotel is the two story building in the center. *Nevada Historical Society.*

the water fast enough. And is the case with many mining camps, stocks were over valued and many investors lost their shirts. By 1865, half the town had moved on to other new strikes.

In 1879, when nearby Bodie boomed, Aurora received rekindled interest. The major mines were reworked. But only four years later, the county seat was moved to Hawthorne; the post office was closed in 1897.

In the early 1900's following the great success of cyanide processing of ore, Jim Cain, a Bodie businessman, purchased the important mines and operated a small mill. Cain leased smaller claims he was not working. In 1912, Jesse Knight's, Aurora Mining Company bought out Cain. Knight erected a cyanide plant and a 40 stamp mill with a 500 ton per day capacity. Shops, warehouses, cottages and bunkhouses were built in a new town called Mangum over the hill from Aurora. Liquor was prohibited in Mangum which caused many new saloons to open in Aurora. These included the Hermitage Bar, Tunnel Saloon, Aurora Club, Northern, Elite Bar, and the First and Last Chance Saloon.

In 1914, Knight sold his interests to the Goldfield Consolidated Mining Company which completed construction of the cyanide plant and worked the mines until 1917 when operations were shut down. The mill, plant and buildings were dismantled and sold. Foundations of the Mangum mill can still be seen today.

By 1920, Aurora had a handful of residents. The town was eventually deserted and stripped. After 1946, Aurora's fine brick buildings were torn down and the bricks were sold. Foundations of mills and buildings, a cemetery and mine sites are all that remains. Still, Aurora is worth a visit, especially if you enjoy rich, blue skies and quiet summer days high in the pine nut mountains.

This is the Syndicate Mill at Bodie. The Real Del Monte Mill located several miles up Bodie Creek probably look similar to this mill. Foundations of the Real Del Monte Mill can be found today. *Courtesy Frank Wedertz.*

The abandoned Aurora buildings in the late 1920's. The Esmeralda Hotel is the two story building in the upper left.

CHAPTER THREE

Sam Goes To Aurora

Sam Clemens arrived in Aurora around April 10, 1862. He was in Aurora for five months, leaving in early October. His stay in Aurora would be one of the most important periods in his life for several reasons.

First, he would gain firsthand experience as a prospector and silver miner. He would learn all about the glory and hell of the prospector's life. For the most part, he would get over the idea of getting rich quick as a miner and investor. Mining experience and knowledge of mining camp life would prepare Clemens for his job as reporter for the *Territorial Enterprise* at Virginia City.

Second, his Aurora mining experiences would provide much interesting and useful material for his second book, *Roughing It*.

Last, boredom and failure as a silver miner would cause Clemens to turn to writing once again. His "Josh" stories, the humorous tales of a hardluck miner's life based on his Aurora experiences, which Clemens wrote at Aurora and were published by the *Territorial Enterprise*, would help him land his first full time writing job. This job would permanently change the course of his life.

Aurora, then, was an important transition phase in Clemens' adult life.

Arriving in Aurora, Clemens, who preferred doing things with others rather than by himself, teamed with Horatio Phillips, the young man who gave Clemens 50 feet in the "Black Warrior" claim. Clemens and Phillips became mining partners and shared a cabin together. After several months, the two had a falling out. Clemens later teamed with

Cal Higbie, Dan Twing and Bob Howland. Mark Twain did not mention Horatio Phillips in *Roughing It*.

Though it was April, it sometimes snows in this high mountain area as late as June. This particular spring the snowfall was unusually heavy. The first thing Clemens and Horatio had to do was find a suitable shelter. They discovered a cabin in Chinatown. The reason it was cheap was because it *was* in Chinatown, a less desireable place.

Sam figured the low price of the cabin was worth the trouble of hauling it from Chinatown up the hill. Sam and Horatio persuaded their friends to help them move the cabin. After a lot of grunts and groans and several hours labor, the men had moved the cabin uptown. Once the cabin was in place their friends cornered Sam and Horatio and made them buy the helpers drinks at the nearest saloon. Buying rounds was so costly, Sam later figured out it would have been cheaper to have bought a more expensive cabin uptown rather than have the cheaper cabin moved.

After the boys were settled in their new cabin, Sam began his mining business. He learned that the mining claims Orion and he had purchased in the fall were worthless. Nor was there further mention of the "Black Warrior" claim, which Horatio Phillips had given Sam interest in.

During his six months at Aurora, Clemens was primarily concerned with five claims: the Dashaway, the Flyaway, the Monitor, the Horatio and Derby and the Annipolitan. In his first letter to Orion written April 13, he reported that the Horatio and Derby was still buried in snow though he hoped to begin working the claim in three or four weeks. The undeveloped claim was already worth $30 to $50 a foot in California. Heavy snow would become a persistent obstacle for Sam's prospecting efforts that spring.

In his first letter, Sam told Orion the status of their various claims:

The "Red Bird" is probably good — can't work on the tunnel account of the snow. The "Pugh" I have thrown away — Shan't re-locate it. It is nothing but bed-rock croppings — too much work to find the ledge, if there is one. Shan't record the "Farnum" until I know more about it — perhaps not at all ... "Governor" under the snow ... "Douglas" & "Red Bird" are both recorded ... Stint yourself as much as possible, and lay up $100 or $150, subject to my call. I go to work tomorrow, with pick and shovel. Something's got to come by G--, before I let go, here.

This wooden cabin photographed at Aurora around 1909, was claimed by some to have been Mark Twain's cabin. It was moved to Reno in the 1920's where it was eventually destroyed by vandals. However, Hank Blanchard, who operated the toll road between Aurora and Bodie and who lived in the area for many years, claimed the original Mark Twain cabin was sold to tourists stick by stick years earlier. This cabin was probably not Mark Twain's cabin but a reasonable example of an Aurora miner's cabin. *Photo by A.A. Forbes.*

33

Sam and Orion also owned the "Live Yankee." Evidently, Orion had not sent Sam the deed to the "Live Yankee." Sam asked Orion to send the deed by mail rather than by the Wells Fargo Express which was very expensive. Mail was delivered once a week from Carson. The Wells Fargo Express delivered letters and packages once a day. Though a letter shipped via Wells Fargo arrived quicker, the cost was quite high. You had to pay Wells Fargo at Carson City and pay twice for the same letter at Aurora. Sam repeatedly told Orion to send papers by mail rather than the more expensive Wells Fargo. For some reason, Orion did not understand this. Sam became angry with Orion for sending mail by the more expensive Wells Fargo.

In this first letter to Orion, Sam also wrote of Indian troubles. Apparently, the Paiute Indians had stolen cattle and killed a man named Scott, the Sherriff and another man. Troops were called in to apprehend the Indians. A skirmish between the Indians and the soldiers resulted in the deaths of Col. Mayfield, Sergeant Gillespie and the wounding of a corporal. The cattle were retrieved. An officer Noble took charge of the stock and was driving the cattle to Aurora.

As with any mining town, troubles over claim jumping often erupted in violence. Sam wrote, "Man named Gebhart shot here yesterday trying to defend a claim on Last Chance Hill. Expect he will die."

Toward the end of his first letter to Orion, Sam laid out his intentions, "I mean to make or break here within 2 or 3 months." But Clemens, always reluctant to quit a project once seriously begun, would stay in Aurora three months longer than planned.

In Aurora less than a week, Sam was having his eyes opened regarding the value of mining properties. April 17 he wrote Orion:

> ... don't buy any ground, anywhere. The pick and shovel are the only claims I have any confidence in now. My back is sore and my hands are blistered with handling them to-day. But something must come, you know ... If I can dig pay rock out of a ledge here myself, I will buy — but not otherwise.

Already he was learning how absentee investors were cheated. A common ploy was for mining companies to levy hefty assessments — bills which had to be paid, the money of which was supposed to be used for mining developments. Often mining companies lived off the assessments never intending to develop the mine. Sam wrote Orion:

34

The "Live Yankees," as you call them, are a pack of d--d fools. They have run a tunnel 100 ft. long to strike the <u>croppings.</u> They could have blasted, above ground, easier. It is the craziest piece of work I know of, except that wherein the owners of the "Esmeralda" discovery sold one-half their interests to get money to run a seventeen-thousand dollar tunnel in, to strike the ledge just under the croppings, when said croppings are 100 feet high ...

In *Roughing It,* Mark Twain elaborated:

Esmeralda [Aurora] was in many respects another Humboldt, but in a little more forward state. The claims we had been paying assessments on were entirely worthless, and we threw them away. The principal one cropped out of the top of a knoll that was fourteen feet high and the inspired Board of Directors were running a tunnel under that knoll to strike the ledge. The tunnel would have to be seventy feet long, and would then strike the ledge at the same depth that a shaft twelve feet deep would have reached! The Board were living on the "assessments" ... The Board had no desire to strike the ledge, knowing that it was as barren of silver as a curbstone. This ... calls to mind Jim Townsend's tunnel. He had paid assessments on a mine called the "Daley" till he was well-nigh penniless. Finally an assessment was levied to run a tunnel two hundred and fifty feet on the Daley, and Townsend went up on the hill to look into matters. He found the Daley cropping out of the apex of an exceedingly sharp-pointed peak, and a couple of men up there "facing" the proposed tunnel. Townsend made a calculation. Then he said to them:

"So you have taken a contract to run a tunnel into this hill two hundred and fifty feet to strike this ledge?"

"Yes, sir."

"Well, do you know that you have got one of the most expensive and arduous undertakings before you that was ever conceived by man?"

"Why no — how is that?"

"Because this hill is only twenty-five feet through from side to side; and so you have got to build two hundred and twenty-five feet of your tunnel on trestle-work!"

The ways of silver mining Boards are exceedingly dark and sinuous.

The Aurora Cemetery is tucked under pine nut trees a half mile from the ghost town.

In Aurora little more than a week, Sam wondered whether he had made the right move. He wrote Billy Claggett at Unionville:

As far as I can see, there are not more than half a dozen leads here that will do to bet on — only two, in fact, that a man would risk his whole pile on. Still, money will be made here as soon as $25-rock can be crushed for $10 a ton. I discover that top-rock which assays $40 is considered "bully." But the large majority of the ledges wouldn't assay $5 on top — the large majority, I think. I know, also, that I own several such. Now I wouldn't give a d--n for any such claims ... Billy, if I hadn't started in here, I would clear out for Humboldt immediately. But since I have got interests here, I will hold on a little, and see if I can make anything out of them. Billy, I told you I would get some claims here, and I could do it, without any trouble; but it strikes me that the fewer feet you own here, the richer you will be. You see, if you fail to do 2 days' work on each claim every month in the year, your property is jumpable at the first instance of neglect.

As at Unionville, buying and selling claims seemed to be where the money was made and many were trying to unload their claims. Sam tells Billy:

Last summer, Orion paid $50 for 15 feet in a claim here. Yesterday one of the owners came and offered me 25 feet more for $50 with 30 days' time on half the amount. He said he hated to part with it, but then he wanted me to have a good "stake." I told him I appreciated his kindness to me, but that I was "on the sell" myself — that I would like to sell him 15 feet at $1 a foot — $2 down, and the balance in thirteen annual installments. Now, do you imagine that he took me up? No by a d--d sight, my love Oh, Shighte! (see Webster,). Tom and I can take a deck of cards, and my old black horse, and win feet enough from Sam in an hour to buy all Esmeralda. There are 5 or 6 leads here, but I am lucky enough not to own in them ...

Sam and Horatio, like hundreds of others, had their own secret scheme through which they believed they would become rich. The scheme involved a man named Clayton, who owned a stamp mill.

Clayton supposedly had discovered a secret milling process which could extract a greater percentage of the gold and silver. Sam told Billy:

... Phillips and I have a project on foot that may amount to something. Mr. Clayton, who uses a "process" of his own, unknown to any one else, saves $300 a ton out of rock from the "Esmeralda" lode — about four times as much as any other mill in the camp can get out of it. He saves silver within 4 percent, and gold within 20 per cent of the fire assay. This he guarantees. He has promised to teach his secret to Phillips (allowing him to teach it to me,) free of charge — and if we use it we are to pay him one-fourth of our profits. And, since you will share with me in this thing, I advise you before-hand not to sell out [at Humboldt]. Now, Billy, you understand why I want to stay here until I get some money out of these d--d leads, if the thing be possible. Because, you see, we want to attach this process to one of your Humboldt mills, and machinery ... will cost us $1,000 to do it with. Keep this entirely to yourself, you know. Clayton will assist us by experimenting with our infernal rock at half-price until we get some that will pay. We haven't taken any out yet that will even do to experiment with. My love to Dad [Mr. Tillou] and the boys ... Don't let my opinion of this place get abroad. Do as I am doing now, Billy — Keep out of leads unless you know them to be good.

April 24, Sam received a letter from Orion which greatly angered him. Orion had meddled with their mining affairs by bankrolling a prospector. Sam was livid; Orion had promised Sam that he would leave all mining matters to him. He wrote Orion:

... You have promised me that you would leave all mining matters, and everything involving an outlay of money, in my hands. Now it may be a matter of no consequence at all to you, to keep your word with me, but I assure you I look upon it in a very different light. Indeed I fully expect you to deal as conscientiously with me as you would with any other man. Moreover, you know as well as I do, that the very best course that you and I can pursue will be, to keep on good terms with each other — notwithstanding which fact we shall certainly split inside of six months if you go

on this way. You see I talk plainly. Because I know what is due me, and I would not put up with such treatment from anybody but you. We discussed that Harroun business once before, and it was <u>decided,</u> then, that he was not to receive a cent of money. But you have paid him $50. And you agreed to pay a portion of Perry's expenses ... all that money you might expend in that project would go to the devil without ever benefitting you a penny ... But as for all the ledges he can find between now and next Christmas, I would not supply his trip with lucifer matches for a half interest in them.

Sending a man fooling around the country after <u>ledges,</u> [ore bearing strata] for God's sake! When there are hundreds of feet of them under my nose here, begging for owners, free of charge. G-d d-n it, I <u>don't want</u> any more feet, and I won't <u>touch</u> another foot — so you see, Orion, as far as any ledges of Perry's are concerned, (or any <u>other</u> except what I examine with my own two eyes,) I freely yield my right to share ownership with you.

Now, Orion, I have given you a piece of my mind — you have it in full, and you deserved it — for you would be ashamed to acknowledge that you ever broke faith with another man as you have with me. I shall never look upon Ma's face again, or Pamela's, or get married, or revisit the "Banner State," until I am a rich man — so you can easily see that when you stand between me and my fortune (the one which I shall make, as surely as Fate itself,) you stand between me and <u>home,</u> friends, and all that I care for — and by the Lord God! you must clear the track, you know!

True to his promise, Sam Clemens did not see his mother again nor did he marry until he was successful. Orion, after Sam's chastising, apparently did not interfere with the mining business again.

Along with the upsetting news, Orion had sent Sam $50.

The next morning Sam attached a postscript:

... I am on my way now, with picks, etc., to work on my pet claim. If it proves good, you will know all about it some day — if it don't you will never even learn its name ... I have Resolved, That it is like most Esmeralda ledges, viz: worthless.

Sam and Horatio continued digging and blasting their tunnel in the

"Horatio and Derby." They still had not reached the ledge they were searching for but it pleased Sam to know that the claim was highly sought after. In California, the Horatio and Derby was selling for $30-50 a foot. Sam told Orion about a man who just had to have part of the claim:

Raish [Horatio] sold a man 30 feet, yesterday, at $20 a foot, although I was present at the sale, and told the man the ground wasn't worth a d--n. He said he had been hankering after a few feet in the H. & D. for a long time, and he had got them at last, and he couldn't help thinking he had secured a good thing. We went and looked at the ledges and both of them acknowledged that there was nothing in them but good "indications."

Clemens, highly intuitive, was beginning to fear that the developing of the Horatio and Derby would swallow more money than it could provide. He wrote Orion, "When you receive your next 1/4rs salary, don't send any of it here until after you have told me you have got it. Remember this. I am afraid of the H. & D."

Toward the end of the April 24th letter, Sam complained about not receiving his commission for Aurora Deputy Sheriff from Carson City. Evidently, the part time job would have given Sam a small but important salary. However, there was a dispute as to whether Aurora was in Nevada or California. Both claimed ownership. Until the dispute was settled, Nevada officials were reluctant to hire a Deputy Sheriff.

Sam concluded his letter on a down note, "Couldn't go on the hill today. It snows. It *always* snows here, I expect."

But four days later, April 28, Sam wrote Orion that they were back to work exploring a new claim, the "Dashaway." Sam wrote Orion:

I have been at work all day, blasting and picking and d--ning one of our new claims — the "Dashaway," — which I don't think a great deal of, but which I am willing to try. We are down, now, 10 or 12 feet. We are following down, <u>under</u> the ledge, but not taking it out. If we get up a windlass tomorrow, we shall take out the ledge, and see whether it is worth anything or not.

The gold and silver ore would be located in the ledge. Mining was a laborious hunt-and-see and there was no easy way to discover whether

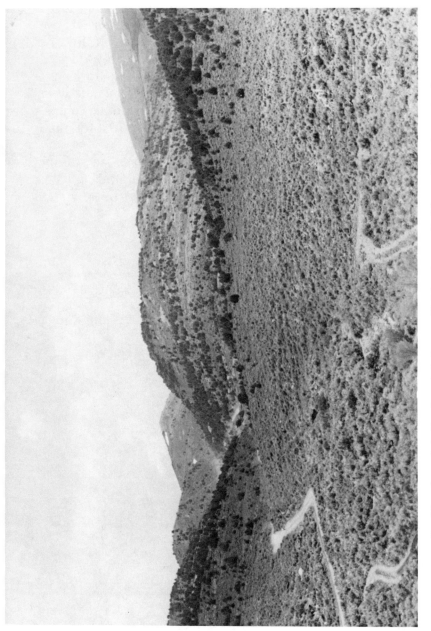

Looking down into the deserted Aurora Gulch where a thriving mining town stood and thousands once lived.

a ledge of quartz was rich without ripping and blasting the ground apart.

Toward the end of this April 28th letter, Clemens told Orion, "I have attended to Barstow." Barstow was the business manager for the *Territorial Enterprise* at Virginia City. Clemens probably queried Barstow about submitting articles for money. Clemens began to submit his "Josh" stories to the *Enterprise* not long after this. These were humorous stories about a hard-luck miner's life in the mining camps. The Josh stories would eventually help Clemens land his first full time reporting job on the *Territorial Enterprise*.

As April ended, Sam had completed his initiation as an Aurora prospector and miner. Now in May, Sam's reason would take a back seat as his emotions ran away with visions of great fortunes.

This is a small stamp mill. Ore fell through a shute into the battery where heavy steel stamps crushed the rock. The crushed ore was then mixed with water, mercury and other chemicals in large vats. Mercury amalgamated with the gold and silver and was later separated. *Courtesy Frank Wedertz.*

CHAPTER FOUR

Aurora Takes Hold Of Sam and His Money

In May, Clemens became more intensely involved with his Aurora mining claims. He and Horatio continued developing a tunnel in the Horatio and Derby but the work was going slow. The hard, monotonous work of digging and blasting a tunnel was making Clemens restless. He did not enjoy hard, manual labor.

Clemens and Horatio purchased shares of two additional claims, the "Flyaway" and the "Monitor." The "Flyaway" cost them $100, $50 down, $50 on time. Afterwards, Sam wrote, they didn't have, "a cent in the house." Sam's pleas to Orion for more money were insistent, "If you can spare $100 conveniently, let me have it — or $50, anyhow."

May 11, Sam wrote Orion:

> I own _one-eighth_ of the new "Monitor Ledge, Clemens Company," and money can't buy a foot of it; because I _know_ it contains our fortune. The ledge is 6 feet wide, and one needs no glass [magnifying glass] to see gold & silver in it. Phillips and I own one-half of a segregated claim in the "Flyaway" discovery, and good interests in two extensions on it. We put men to work on our part of the discovery yesterday, and last night they brought us some fine specimens. Rock taken from 10 feet below the surface on the other part of the discovery _has_ yielded $150.00 to the ton, in the mill and we are at work 300 feet from their shaft.

May 12, Horatio began working with Clayton, the mill owner, learning his secret milling process. Clemens and Horatio must have truly believed in Clayton's secret process. For where other mills were charging milling fees of $18 a ton, Clayton was charging $50.

Clemens was now convinnced that their two new claims, the Flyaway and the Monitor would produce fortunes for the partners. He wrote Orion May 12:

> *When you and I came out here, we did not expect '63 or '64 to find us rich men — and if that proposition had been made, we would have accepted it gladly. Now it is made ... if all spare change be devoted to working the "Monitor and the "Flyaway," 12 months, or 24 at furthest, will find all our earthly wishes satisfied, so far as money is concerned...*

Be that as it was, Sam and Horatio were living at the edge of poverty:

> *Raish is looking anxiously for money, and so am I. Send me whatever you can spare conveniently — and if you own nothing on the Dayton lots, sell one of them for $100, or both for $150, if you can do no better, and can't otherwise raise that amount conveniently. I want it to work the Flyaway with. My fourth of that claim only cost me $50, (which isn't paid yet, though,) and I suppose I could sell it here in town for ten times that amount, to-day, but I shall probably hold on to it till the cows come home. I shall work the "Monitor" and the other claims with my own hands.*

By mid-May, Aurora was beginning to over-flow with new arrivals. Each day the stage brought in 25-30 newcomers. The town buzzed with excitement as strike after new strike was announced and praised. Nearly every man believed he would be rich — or at least believed he could be rich within a short period.

Clemens, not unlike others, was consumed. Convinced his three claims would make he and Orion wealthy, he asked Orion for more money to pour down Aurora's empty holes. Though it was still snowing in mid-May, Sam was determined to stick it out:

> *... I have struck my tent in Esmeralda, [Aurora] and I care for no mines but those which I can superintend myself. I am a citizen*

*here now, and I am satisfied — although R. [Horatio] and I are
"strapped" and we haven't three days' rations in the house.*

Clemens and Horatio, like other miners, had reached a cash flow crisis. They had spent all their money purchasing and developing tunnels but had not received a return on their investments.

May 17, Sam received another $100 from Orion. With money in his hands, he was ready to gamble it all — and more, on the Flyaway. He wrote Orion:

*Stand by, now, for we shall let a contract on the Flyaway to-
morrow, which will cost about $100 — sink a shaft 25 feet deep
... The cards are the Flyaway and the Monitor — and we will stake
the whole pile on them. If they win, we are all right — if they
lose, I am busted.*

Here Clemens exhibited one of his most positive character traits: his ability to risk all for the long shot. Risk taking would greatly help Clemens to succeed as a writer and businessman.

But as if life at Aurora wasn't tough enough, matters grew worse. The Monitor claim was jumped! Sam wrote Orion:

*Two or three of the old "Salina" company entered our hole on
the Monitor yesterday morning, before our men got there, and
took possession, armed with revolvers. And according to the d--d
laws of this forever d--d country nothing but the District Court
(and there ain't any) can touch the matter, unless it assumes the
shape of an infernal humbug which they call "forcible entry and
detainer," and in order to bring that about, you must compel the
jumpers to use personal violence toward you! We went up and
demanded possession, and they refused. Said they were in the hole,
armed and meant to die in it if necessary. I got in it with them,
and again demanded possession. They said I might stay in it as
long as I pleased, and work but they would do the same. I asked
one of our company to take my place in the hole, while I went
to consult a lawyer. He did so. The lawyer said it was no go. They
must offer some "force."*

*Our boys will try to be there first in the morning — in which
case they may get possession and keep it. Now you understand*

This mining deed, dated March 1, 1862, is the first recorded deed of Aurora mining claims Sam Clemens purchased from John Kinney. Clemens had purchased interests in the "Allamoocha," "Scioto," "Winnemucca," "Ottowa," "Tom Thumb," "Fresno," "Horatio," "Carrie Conoon," "Rosetta," "Potomac," "Boston," and "Longfellow," all of which proved worthless.

the shooting scrape in which Gebhart was killed the other day. The Clemens Company, [Sam's mining company] all of us — hate to resort to arms in this matter, and it will not be done until it becomes a forced hand — but I think that will be the end of it, nevertheless.

Imagine the scene. Here is young Sam Clemens, the future great American author, Mark Twain, risking his life to defend his rights to a hole in the ground! Clemens had placed himself in a very dangerous position by confronting the claim jumpers. Daily, men were killed and wounded over mining claims. Clemens could have easily become another statistic.

Sam and Horatio sued the Monitor claim jumpers in court. By June 2, the Monitor dispute was settled. Sam and Horatio essentially won though they were forced to give a small portion of the Monitor to the claim jumpers. Clemens was apparently satisfied.

Sometime in May, Clemens began submitting his "Josh" stories to the *Enterprise,* then the most important voice in the Territory and one of the most outstanding papers on the West Coast. Clemens was surprised when the *Enterprise* published his letters. None of these letters have survived but they were evidently clever enough to catch the attention of Joe Goodman, editor of the *Enterprise*. In time the letters would help Clemens land a reporting job on the *Enterprise*.

In his May 17, letter to Orion, Clemens first wrote of his affiliation with the *Enterprise*. "I hope Barstow [of the *Enterprise*] wil leave the "S.L.C." off my Gate City letters, in case he publishes them. Put my *Enterprise* letters in the scrap book — but send no extracts from them *East.*" This makes it clear that Clemens was already submitting his Josh letters to the *Enterprise* and they were being published.

But Clemens was more interested in his mines and Clayton's secret milling process than writing. He told Orion:

Mr. Clayton seems inclined to help us all he can. I saw him yesterday, and he said that in the course of 5 or 6 weeks he expected to commence teaching me the process, and when I have learned it, he wants Raish and me to go out to Humboldt, get it used by Humboldt Mills, and stay there and work it. As soon as I commence learning it, I shall write to Billy C. [Claggett] to begin puffing it up out there.

Despite his enthusiasm and great faith, by early June, Sam's money situation still had not improved. "We haven't money enough to work the "Flyaway," so, we shall hold on and see if we can financier it out without cash," he told Orion. He only had $25 dollars left and complained that it cost $8-10 a week to "batch in this d--d place. Send me all the money you can spare every week or so, without further orders." This amount may not seem much to a modern reader but at this time, a laborer worked ten hour days, five days a week for $20 — and this was considered good pay! Eight or ten dollars a week, then, would have been half a laborers pay, and since Sam was self-employed, he received no wages except for the money Orion supplied him.

But Sam's visions of wealth gave him hope. June 2 he wrote Orion that he and Horatio had secured 200 feet of a 400 foot claim which adjoined the Wide West, a rich gold mine. They named their new claim, the "Annipolitan." The Annipolitan would be the closest Clemens would come to striking it rich.

Remains of a toll station at the California-Nevada border in Bodie Canyon near Aurora.

CHAPTER FIVE

The Annipolitan and the Wide West Mine

In *Roughing It*, Mark Twain told the famous story of how he and Cal Higbie were millionaires for a week. According to Twain's fictionalized account, he and Higbie discovered that a spur of the rich Wide West gold mine was a "blind lead." A blind lead is a separate vein not claimed by the original locators. This meant that he and Higbie could file a claim on the blind lead and take possession, which they did. According to Twain, the blind lead was extraordinarily rich in gold and there was no doubt that they were millionaires.

There was only one catch: to retain possession of the blind lead, they were required to do development work on the claim within ten days. In Twain's story, he and Higbie failed to do the required work and lost title to the Wide West blind lead and thereby lost their fortunes.

Twain's fictionalized story twisted the facts for the sake of a good story. The real story goes like this:

June 2, Sam wrote Orion that he and Horatio had purchased 200 feet of a 400 foot claim which adjoined the Wide West, a rich gold mine. Sam and Horatio's shaft was 100 feet from the Wide West shaft. There was good reason to believe that their claim, which they named the Annipolitan, would also be rich in gold.

June 9, Sam wrote that he and Horatio traded half of their share in the Annipolitan, 100 feet, in exchange for the work of laborers who dug a 30 foot shaft into the Annipolitan. In addition, they paid $36 for blasting powder and tools.

By June 22, Sam and Horatio had shifted their interest from the

Monitor to the Flyaway and the Annipolitan. Sam and Horatio hired men to sink shafts in both claims.

Sam excitedly explained to Orion that a rich gold strike was made in the "Pride of Utah" which adjoined their Annipolitan claim and the Wide West mine:

> The "Annipolitan" shaft is about 200 feet from the P. [Pride] of Utah and Dines-W.W. [Wide West] shafts. These two ledges are so close together that I don't see how ours could be crowded between them — and we are most damnably "mixed" as to whether the "Annipolitan" will prove to be the "Dines" or the "Pride of Utah." We want it to be the former — for in that case we can hold our ground — but if it be the "Pride of Utah," we shall lose all of it except fifty feet, as the "P. of U." was located first. There is an extension on the "P. of U.," and in order to be on the safe side, we have given them notice not to work on it. We are in a good neighborhood, for, since the rich strikes on the "Dines" and "Pride of Utah," they have resumed work on the "W.W." incline, and are getting out very handsome rock. McNear, who owns one-half the "Annipolitan," says he would not sell an inch for even $2,000 a foot. He is the best pleased man I know. Well, it _does_ seem like a dead sure thing, — but then its the d--dest country for disappointments the world ever saw.

All of this may be confusing if you do not have knowledge of mining laws of that era. From what Clemens has written, the Dines claim could be the answer to their prayers. If the Annipolitan spur is mixed with the Dines claim, Sam and Horatio would be permitted to retain ownership of their claim and work it. However, if the Annipolitan is mixed with the Pride of Utah mine, Sam and Horatio would lose all their ground except for 50 feet because the Pride of Utah was "located," or filed on, first. The Annipolitan was located in a very good area. The Dines, Pride of Utah and Wide West had struck rich ledges. The question now was, would the Annipolitan be part of the Dines or the Pride of Utah? The answer would determine whether or not Sam and Horatio would retain ownership.

As Clemens waited to learn whether or not they would retain ownership of the Annipolitan, it was clear he was growing impatient for something good to break. He wrote Orion June 22:

50

...I am mighty impatient to see the shaft down on the "A," [Annipolitan] — but if 30 feet don't find it rich, we will sink 30 more immediately — so I expect to be here 3 months longer, anyhow. I have now been here over two months ... but I know, and you know, that I cannot double that time in any one place without a miracle — I have been here as long, now, as it is in my nature to stay in one place — and from this out I shall feel as much like a prisoner as if I were in the county jail. I believe I have not spent six months in one place — since 1853 ... and God knows I want to be moving to-day ... Christ! how sick I am of these same old humdrum scenes.

Remains of a mill just outside of Aurora. Builders used the local rock to build the foundations of many buildings.

This deed dated August 1, 1862, shows that Cal Higbie sold a portion of the Annipolitan mining claim to Sam Clemens for $500.

Esmeralda, June 22, 1862.

My Dear Bro:

Things are going on pretty much as usual. Our men are still at work on the "Annipolitan" and "Flyaway," but we are doing nothing on the "Monitor," as the other parties have until the end of this month to appear in. They have struck it fully as rich in the "Pride of Utah" as in the "Wide West." Here is the position of the ledges:

You see the grand rock comes from the "Dimes," in reality, and not from the W. W. although the latter said nothing about it until they had bought into the former. The "Annipolitan" shaft is about 200 feet from the P. of Utah and Dimes–W. W. shafts. These two ledges are so close together that I don't see how ours could be crowded between them — and we are most damnably "mixed" as to whether the "Annipolitan" will prove to be the "Dimes" or the "Pride of Utah." We want it to be the former — for, in that case we can hold all our ground —

The first page of Sam Clemens' June 22, 1862 letter to Orion. Sam drew a picture to help explain where the promosing Annipolitan claim was located. *Samuel L. Clemens Collection, Clifton Waller Barrett Library, University of Virginia Library.*

53

As for his writing, by his June 22 letter, it is clear that the *Enterprise* had published several of his "Josh" stories. He told Orion, "Put all Josh's letters in my scrap book, I may have use for them some day. As he would in later years, Clemens complained that the *Enterprise* printers had incorrectly typeset his last Josh letter. "Those *Enterprise* fellows make perfect nonsense of my letters. Like all d--d fool printers, they can't follow the punctuation as it is in the manuscript. They have, by this means made a mass of senseless d--d stupidity of my last letter." Clemens, for all his humor, was a serious and deliberate man. His complaint about the *Enterprise* printers, shows that Clemens, even at this point, took his writing seriously and desired his manuscripts to be correctly translated to the reader. Over his long career, Clemens bitterly complained about editors who hacked his manuscripts and printers who changed his carefully considered punctuation without consulting him.

There was other news about his writing, "I have quit writing for the "Gate." [Gate City] I haven't got time to write. I half intended writing east to-night, but I hardly think I will."

By July 9, Clemens was already planning ahead for the winter. He would need some sort of work and was beginning to seriously consider newspaper writing. William Gillespie, a friend of Orion's who was trying to start a newspaper, was interested in Sam writing for the paper. Sam wrote Orion about the position:

> *Tell him [Gillespie] not to secure a San Francisco correspondent for the winter, because they do nothing here during the winter months, and I want the job myself. I want to spend the winter in California. When will his first number be published and where?*
>
> *Tell Church I would as soon write a correspondence for the [Carson] "Age" as not, since Lewis is out of the concern, but want of time will not permit it. Besides, I have no private room, and it is a torture to write where there is a crowd around, as is the case here, always.*

By July 9, the mystery over Sam's highly valued Annipolitan claim was solved. The Annipolitan spur was mixed with the Pride of Utah claim which meant Sam and Horatio's shares in the Annipolitan were worthless. It was very bad news. Clemens hopes of striking it rich in Aurora were seriously damaged. From this point on, Clemens would be preparing for his next move.

CHAPTER SIX

Sam and the Lost Cement Gold Mine

After the disappointment with the Annipolitan claim, Clemens was disgusted with Aurora. His mining investments had cost hundreds of dollars and much wasted time. He was sick of being cooped up at Aurora. He wanted to get away for a rest and to investigate other mining possibilities in the vicinity. Though it was early July, Clemens would be in and out of Aurora until September 9. He would do no further serious mining at Aurora. Clemens would spend the last two months making several exploratory trips around the Mono Lake area, learning Clayton's secret milling process and vacationing before he left Aurora for Virginia City.

July 9, Sam wrote Orion, "I caught a violent cold at Clayton's, [while learning his secret milling process] which lasted two weeks, and I came near getting salivated, working in the quicksilver and chemicals. I hardly think I shall try the experiment again. It is a confining business, and will not be confined, for love nor money." Quick silver, or mercury, was used in the milling process. Free silver and gold are easily collected by the quick silver. Working with mercury is very dangerous. The fumes can make a person dangerously ill and can kill. Clemens evidently discovered this for himself.

Shortly after the Annipolitan disappointment, Sam and Horatio Phillips parted company. Sam wrote Orion July 23:

> *At any rate, with regard to Phillips ... He is a d--d rascal, and I can get the signatures of 25 men to this sentiment whenever I*

want them. He shall not be paid out of the Record fund. Tell him if he can't wait for the money, he can have his ground back, and welcome — that is, 12 1/2 feet of it — or 25, for that matter, for it isn't worth a d--n, except that the work on it will hold until the next great convulsion of nature injects gold and silver into it.

Clemens then teamed with Cal Higbie, to whom he dedicated *Roughing It.* In his letter of July 9, to Orion, Sam first mentioned Cal Higbie.

Higbie is a large, strong man, and has the perseverance of the devil ... You can no more discourage him than you can frighten him. Visiting the Yo-Semite Falls, (100 miles from here,) he carried for two-thirds of a day, a 60-pound pack on his back, and a rifle and shot-gun in his hands, and then left the valley and climbed to the summit of the ridge, (which is 7,000 feet above the valley,) by a trail, which the mountain goats are almost afraid of.

In his fictionalized story of the Wide West mine, Mark Twain wrote that Cal Higbie was a partner, though in reality his partner during the Annipolitan episode was Horatio Phillips.

Not much is known of Higbie. He was an honest, forthright man who had evidently spent considerable time in the mining camps. By the number of misspelled words in a letter Higbie wrote to Mark Twain years later, we learn he was not well educated.

Clemens' teaming with Higbie was important. Higbie knew the Mono Lake area well and led Clemens to various areas on exploration trips. It was with Higbie that Clemens first visited Mono Lake. And it was through Higbie that Clemens became involved with Gid Whiteman's lost cement gold mine which Mark Twain wrote of in *Roughing It.*

There are several stories of the legendary lost cement gold mine. The mine was said to be located near Mono Lake at the headwaters of the Owens River. During the summer of 1862, Whiteman's lost cement gold mine caused a great excitement at Aurora.

First, let's clarify the word "cement." The word here means a sort of conglomerate rock throughout which, "lumps of virgin gold ... thick ... as raisins," as Twain wrote, were embedded. Clemens, like other Aurora miners, saw samples from the legendary gold mine and was astounded by its richness. For many years a sample of the cement mine

A rare photograph of Cal Higbie, one of Clemens' mining partners at Aurora. Twain dedicated *Rouging It* to Cal Higbie. Sam Clemens and Higbie were nearly killed while making a visit to Paoha Island at Mono Lake. *Special Collections, University of Nevada, Reno.*

gold was exhibited in Aurora at Chapin's, later Frank Schoenmaker's saloon.

Like many lost gold mine tales, the story is based on some facts and on real people who can be traced and documented. There are several versions of the tale but the one which holds up best is this one:

An emigrant party was on their way to California on the southern route through Death Valley where the party met disaster. There, two men lost their teams and continued on foot with the party until it reached the Sierra Nevada. Here, the two men left the party to take a shorter route across the mountains.

They traveled through what they called "burnt country," lava fields which are located in southern Inyo County and parts of Mono County near Mono Lake. As the men made their way into the Sierra, they came to the head of a stream believed to be the Owens River, not far from Mono Lake. While resting beside the stream, the men saw a curious rock with gold in it. They pounded the rock and opening it saw so much gold color that they questioned whether or not it was really gold. The men put samples of the rock in their pockets and continued their journey across the Sierra. On the Western slope of the Sierra they found another stream believed to be the middle fork of the San Joaquin River which they followed down to Millertown, the Fresno County seat 1856-74. The men mined at Millertown, failed and separated. One man went to San Francisco where he eventually contracted consumption.

The doctor who attended the man was named Randall. The dying man showed Dr. Randall the gold he had found near the Owens River. He said he learned at Millertown that it was indeed gold, had wished to return to the area but became ill. He paid Dr. Randall with a sample of the gold found at the head of the Owens River. Dying, the man gave Dr. Randall a brief description of the place where he had found the gold and made a rough map of the site.

This was in the fall of 1860. Dr. Randall believed the dying man had told the truth. In addition, he had the rich sample the man gave him. The sample was described by those who saw it as looking like decomposed quartz, reddish-rust colored, strewn with flakes of gold.

The following summer, 1861, Dr. Randall crossed the Sierra to the east side and came to Monoville. Randall searched an area south of Mono Lake near the headwaters of the Owen River for the cement gold mine. Randall located a quarter section of land, 160 acres on Pumice Flat, 37 miles south of Monoville. The local miners considered Randall

This man is pouring liquid gold into a mold to make a gold brick. Photograph taken at the Standard Mill at Bodie around 1909. Notice the steel plates on the floor which prevented molten gold from slipping through the floor. *A.A. Forbes photo.*

A very rare photograph of Bob Howland, one of Clemens' mining partners. Howland was the nephew of Nevada Governor James Nye. Howland later achieved notoriety as Aurora's fearless town marshal. *Photo courtesy of Mr. Robert M. Gunn and the Mark Twain Project.*

a fool for having located Pumice Flat for mining ground.

This area later became known as Whiteman's camp.

Randall returned to the Mono Lake area in the summer of 1862. He employed Gid Whiteman and eleven others who searched the 160 acres. They discovered a ledge of reddish lava type rock embedded with gold. Randall brought a specimen back to Aurora and showed it off. Whether or not it was the original specimen or one he had recently discovered, is uncertain. In any case, Randall's specimen caused a mass exodus of miners from Aurora that summer who searched the area but found nothing.

In early July, Clemens became sort of involved with the lost cement mine. He explains in *Roughing It*:

> *A new partner of ours, a Mr. Higbie, knew Whiteman well by sight, and a friend of ours, a Mr. Van Dorn, [real name was Van Horn] was well acquainted with him, and not only that, but had Whiteman's promise that he should have a private hint in time to enable him to join the next cement expedition. Van Dorn [Van Horn] had promised to extend the hint to us. One evening Higbie came in, greatly excited, and said he felt certain he had recognized Whiteman, uptown, disguised and in a pretended state of intoxication. In a little while Van Dorn arrived and confirmed the news; and so we gathered in our cabin and with our heads close together arranged our plans in impressive whispers.*
>
> *We were to leave town quietly, after midnight, in two or three small parties, so as not to attract attention, and meet at dawn on the "divide" overlooking Mono Lake, eight or nine miles distant.*

Van Horn, a man from Lee Vining, was linked with Gid Whiteman and his search for the lost cement gold mine. Though Van Horn may have given Higbie and Clemens inside information, Higbie left Aurora alone for the cement diggings. July 9, Sam wrote Orion:

> *... last week when the news came, he [Higbie] said nothing, but got a horse, and left here that night at midnight. I had a whispered message from him last night, in which he said he had arrived safely on the ground, and was in with the discoverers, turning the [Owens] river out of its bed. They will allow no others to participate. Higbie left here while I was with Capt. Nye. Now keep all this entirely*

to yourself. Nine-tenths of the people who leave here for the diggings, don't know where to go ... If there is anything there, he [Higbie] will find it. And when he gets discouraged and leaves, rest assured he will leave no one behind him ... I am telling you these things so that if you learn that Higbie calls the new diggings a steamboat [unsubstantial discovery], you can feel convinced that there is no gold in that part of the country. I am freezing for him to send word for me to come out there — for God knows a respite from this same old, old place would be a blessing.

Whether Clemens left Aurora for the cement digging between July 10 and July 22 is doubtful. July 23 he wrote Orion that he planned to make a short trip, "I shall go on a walking tour of 40 or 50 miles shortly, to get rid of this infernal place for a while," but Clemens did not make his walking trip until the first week in August.

And times were still tough. Sam told Orion:

My debts are greater than I thought for. I bought $25 worth of clothing, and sent $25 to Higbie, in the cement diggings. I owe about 45 or $50, and have got $45 in my pocket. But how in the hell I am going to live on something over $100 until October or November, is singular. The fact is, I must have something to do, and that shortly, too. I want that money to pay assessments with. And if Turner [Judge Turner, a prospective buyer] don't accept my offer right away, I'll make a sale of that ground d--d soon. I don't want to sell any of it, though until the Fresno tunnel is in. Then I'll sell the extension ... I want to have a shaft sunk 100 feet on the Monitor, but I am afraid to try it, for want of money.

Running short on money, Sam, like other miners in a pinch, considered selling some of his mining properties. In need of some kind of work, he now seriously considered writing correspondent letters. He told Orion, who apparently had connections with the Sacramento *Union*, to put in a good word for him.

Now write the Sacramento Union folks, or to Marsh, and tell them I'll write as many letters a week as they want, for $10 a week — my board must be paid. Tell them I have corresponded with the N. [New] Orleans Crescent, and other papers — and the

Enterprise. California is full of people who have interests here, and it's d--d seldom they hear from this country. I can't write a specimen letter — [an example of his writing] now, at any rate — I'd rather undertake to write a Greek poem. Tell 'em the mail & express leave here three times a week, and it costs from 25 to 50 cents to send letters by that blasted express. If they want letters from here, who'll run from morning till night collecting materials cheaper. I'll write a short letter twice a week for the present for the [Carson] "Age," for $5 per week. Now it has been a long time since I couldn't make my own living, and it shall be a long time before I loaf another year.

Clemens apparently never went to the cement diggings. Letters he wrote afterward say nothing further of Whiteman's lost mine. However, the excitement that summer over Whiteman's lost cement gold provided Clemens with the basis for another story for *Roughing It*.

As Clemens closed his July 23 letter to Orion he wrote, "And if I can't move the bowels of these hills this fall, I will come up and clerk for you until I get money enough to go over the mountains for winter." But there was something else in store for Sam Clemens and it would not be clerking for Orion.

Another rare photograph of Bob Howland, far left, and his dugout cabin at Aurora. *Courtesy of Robert M. Gunn and the Mark Twain Project.*

Aurora around 1884. A large mill is located on Middle Hill at the upper center of the photograph. Silver Hill, where most mines were located, is on the right. Martinez Hill is at the far left. The central part of town was located in Aurora Gulch through which a small creek flowed in the spring and early summer months. *Nevada Historical Society.*

CHAPTER SEVEN

Sam Explores Mono Lake and Vicinity

Around July 30, Sam Clemens received an offer from William Barstow of the *Enterprise* which would permanently change the course of his life. He wrote Orion, "Barstow has offered me the post of local reporter for the *Enterprise* at $25 a week, and I have written him that I will let him know next mail if possible, whether I can take it or not. If G. [Gillespie] is not sure of starting his paper within a month, I think I had better close with Barstow's offer." A week later, Sam had made up his mind. August 7, he told Orion, "I wrote him [Barstow] that I guessed I would take it, and asked him how long before I must come up there. I have not heard from him since."

Clemens had planned to winter in San Francisco, the largest city on the Coast at that time and a place he had heard much talk of. He had counted on Gillespie starting his paper so he might work in San Francisco as a correspondent. But apparently Gillespie's paper did not get off the ground. And this was good. For Gillespie's paper could have never given Clemens the great opportunity and exposure the *Enterprise* did. Somewhat reluctantly, shuffling his feet, Clemens accepted the reporting post for the *Enterprise*. He had no idea at the time, but his decision to write for the paper was perhaps the most important decision Clemens made during his adult life. His reporting post on the *Enterprise* would lead Clemens to his lifelong career as a serious writer. While writing for the *Enterprise*, Clemens would adopt his famous pen name, Mark Twain.

Without money to work his mining properties, there was nothing for Clemens to do at Aurora. He felt cooped up; he wanted to get away; he wanted a rest; he wanted to go exploring and fishing. August 7, he wrote Orion:

Now, I shall leave at mid-night tonight, alone and on foot for a walk of 60 or 70 miles through a totally uninhabited country, and it is barely possible that mail facilities may prove infernally "slow" during the few weeks I expect to spend out there. But do you write Barstow that I have left here for a week or so, and in case he should want me he must write me here, or let me know through you. You see I want to know something about that country out yonder.

By early August, Cal Higbie had discovered Whiteman's latest diggings were worthless and had either returned to Aurora or gone to Monoville where he may have sent word for Sam to join him. In any case, Clemens left Aurora around August 8 for a week. During this time Clemens explored Mono Lake with Cal Higbie and probably visited Monoville.

The gold mining camp of Monoville was the second important gold strike east of the Sierra and the first settlement between Genoa and the Owens Valley towns. Monoville was located in Rattlesnake Gulch about one mile east of today's Conway Summit on Highway 395 and about 5 miles north of the northwestern shore of Mono Lake. Monoville was about a 25 mile walk from Aurora.

Placer gold was discovered at Monoville in the spring of 1859. Dick and Leroy Vining, for whom the nearby town of Lee Vining is named, were among the first Monoville miners.

In the spring of 1860, hoards of miners crossed the Sierra to Monoville. Monoville served an important historical purpose. Being the only trading center for miles, all the major gold and silver strikes in the area — Aurora, Bodie, and Benton, were made by men who were from Monoville or obtained their provisions there. The men who discovered gold at Aurora were on their way to Monoville when they made their discovery.

At its peak in 1860, Monoville had a population of 500 to 2,000 men. The isolated camp boasted several hotels and about 40 houses, of which only one stone cabin exists today. By April, 1862, following the Aurora excitement, the post office was closed. Most had moved on to Aurora.

In *Roughing It*, Mark Twain wrote, "... we adjourned to the Sierra on a fishing excursion, and spent several days in camp under snowy Castle Peak, and fished successfully for trout in a bright, miniature lake..." The author discovered this lake is Trumboll Lake, located about 5 miles west of Conway Summit on Virginia Lakes road. Trumboll Lake is a popular camping and fishing site today.

Clemens likely visited Monoville during his August vacation while on his way to Trumboll Lake where he fished and camped for about a week. In *Roughing It* he wrote:

At the end of a week we adjourned to the Sierras on a fishing excursion, and spent several days in camp under snowy Castle Peak, and fished successfully for trout in a bright, miniature lake whose surface was between ten and eleven thousand feet above the level of the sea; cooling ourselves during the hot August noons by sitting on snowbanks ten feet deep, under whose sheltering edges fine grass and dainty flowers flourished luxuriously; and at night entertained ourselves by almost freezing to death.

The "miniature lake," Mark Twain wrote of, is Trumboll Lake which is at the southern base of Castle Peak. The lake is about 5 miles from the Monoville site. Today this lake can easily be reached by car from Conway Summit by taking Virginia Lakes road.

Like the Indians and white men with sense, Clemens and Higbie had climbed high into the mountains to escape the August heat.

It was probably after their fishing excursion to Trumboll Lake, that Clemens and Higbie explored the shores of Mono Lake. Mark Twain wrote in *Roughing It*:

We traveled around to a remote and particularly wild spot on the borders of the lake, where a stream of fresh, ice-cold water entered it from the mountainside, and then we went regularly into camp. We hired a large boat and two shotguns from a lonely ranchman who lived some ten miles further on and made ready for comfort and recreation. We soon got thoroughly acquainted with the lake and all its peculiarities.

The site where Clemens and Higbie camped was probably on the northwestern shore near the point where Mill Creek enters Mono Lake. This place is walking distance from today's Mono Lake County Park just west of Black Point. Ranches and farms were located in this area on the well watered grasslands.

During their week's stay at Mono Lake, Sam and Cal Higbie, nearly lost their lives when they ventured out to Paoha Island in a rowboat.

Clemens, probably due to his hard-luck, was not enraptured by the

Our children stand next to the tufa towers at the Tufa Reserve located 4 miles east of the intersection of Highways 395 and 120. *Photo Edie Williams.*

Looking north from the south shore to Paoha Island where Mark Twain and Cal
Higbie nearly lost their lives August, 1862. *Photo Edie Williams.*

Our Children play on Navy Beach building their own mini tufa towers from the beach sand. *Photo Edie Williams.*

beauty of Mono Lake and its dramatic mountain surroundings. He wrote:

> Mono, it is sometimes called, and sometimes the "Dead Sea of California." It is one of the strangest freaks of Nature to be found in any land, but it is hardly ever mentioned in print and very seldom visited, because it lies away off the usual routes of travel and besides is so difficult to get at that only men content to endure the roughest life will consent to take upon themsleves the discomforts of such a trip ... Mono Lake lies in a lifeless, treeless, hideous desert, eight thousand feet above the level of the sea, and is guarded by mountains two thousand feet higher, whose summits are always clothed in clouds. This solemn, silent, sailess sea — this lonely tenant of the loneliest spot on earth — is little graced with the picturesque. It is an unpretending expanse of grayish water, about a hundred miles in circumference, with two islands in its center, mere upheavals of rent and scorched and blistered lava, snowed over with gray banks and drifts of pumice stone and ashes, the winding sheet of the dead volcano, whose vast crater the lake has seized upon and occupied.
>
> *Roughing It*

It was unlike Clemens to miss the beauty of a natural setting. The wasteland he saw in Mono Lake and the surrounding mountains today is a beautiful, awesome sight to many.

Here, east and just over the mountains from Yosemite National Park, is the strange but beautiful Mono Basin, a land of striking contrasts. Bordering the Basin on the west is the Sierra Nevada range snow capped the entire year. To the north are the basalt covered Bodie Hills where gold was discovered at Bodie. To the east are rolling volcanic hills. To the south are the grey domes of the Mono Craters, silent young volcanos which still have the potential of blowing their tops. In the high country above the lake are pine nut trees and Jeffrey Pines. In the lowlands the land is covered with sagebrush which has a pungent, wild fragrance. The northwestern shores are well watered grasslands with wildflowers and willows where ranches and farms once existed.

Black Point, a low, flat peninsula on the north shore, juts into the lake like a huge black toe. The sandy, charred ashes of Black Point, a retired volcano, look as smooth as if God carefully laid his hands and smoothed the once fiery surface.

But perhaps strangest of all, are the great white towers standing at the edge of the lake like frozen white angels, some over twenty feet tall. These are the tufa towers formed over thousands of years by the bubbling up of fresh water springs through the chemical infested waters of Mono Lake. They remind one of stalagmites. Some say they look like huge cauliflower. The tufa towers are one of the strangest and rarest natural wonders.

Mono Lake has two islands, Paoha, the larger tawny colored and Negit, the black lava island. They beckon the curious like the Mississippi River islands of *Tom Sawyer*. Even Clemens found these volcanic islands alluring. On a venture out to Paoha Island he discovered that on the island

> *Nature has provided an unfailing spring of boiling water ... and you can put your eggs in there, and in four minutes you can boil them as hard as any statement I have made during the past fifteen years. Within ten feet of the boiling spring is a spring of pure cold water, sweet and wholesome. So, in that island you get you board and your washing free of charge ...*

Though Clemens considered Mono Lake a lifeless, silent sea, it is teaming with a peculiar but wondrous life. The truth is, between May and October, the shores of Mono Lake are filled with the cries of seagulls and flocks of birds who make Mono Lake an annual breeding ground and rest stop.

Mono Lake, 15 miles south of the Aurora site, lies sprawled out in a great desert basin at about 6,373 feet. The lake is sort of oval shaped, running 13 miles east to west and about eight miles north to south and holds more water than any other lake in California. But it is a strange sort of water, highly alkaline and about three times as salty as the ocean. The heavy concentrations of salts and other chemicals make the water slippery to the touch. The water will sting cuts, abrasions and the eyes. But swimmers float bouyantly on the water and do not sink. Because of the extreme alkalinity, there are no fish in the lake. Brine shrimp and algae are about the only things able to live in this water. And these thrive in astounding numbers which help make Mono Lake part of an important life system.

During the spring and summer, millions of brine shrimp feed on the great quantities of algae. The huge numbers of brine shrimp are food for flocks of migrating birds which use Mono Lake as a sort of vacation paradise.

From May through October, Mono Lake is a bird watcher's heaven as hundreds of thousands of California Gulls, Snowy Plovers, Wilson's Phalaropes, Northern Phalaropes Eared Grebes and others arrive. The birds feed on the brine shrimp and huge numbers of brine flies which form a black ring at the edge of the lake. The birds mate and lay their eggs on Mono Lake's two islands where they are safe from mainland predators, coyotes, racoons, weasels and man. Ninety-five percent of the state's California Gulls nest at Mono Lake.

Therefore, Mono Lake fills an important biological niche in the migratory life of thousands of birds.

Even Twain had to admit:

Providence leaves nothing to go by chance. All things have their uses and their part and proper place in Nature's economy: the ducks eat the flies — the flies eat the worms — the Indians eat all three — the wildcats eat the Indians — the white folks eat the wildcats — and thus all things are lovely.

Rouging It

But the sensitive balance of Mono Lake's unusual ecological system has recently been disturbed by man's intervention.

Until the 1940's, Mono Lake was supplied water by a half dozen streams which flowed freely from the Sierra Nevada into the lake. The largest and most important were Rush Creek and Lee Vining Creek.

Since the 1940's, Los Angeles has diverted Rush and Lee Vining Creeks away from the lake and into an aqueduct which carries the water to the city. These diversions deprived the lake of 80% of its water source causing the lake to drop 45 vertical feet, doubling the salinity of the lake. The shrinking of the lake caused a land bridge to form between the northern shore and Negit Island. The land bridge enabled mainland predators to reach Negit Island where large numbers of chicks were killed. Negit Island became unsafe and the birds would no longer nest there. This caused a severe drop in hatchlings.

A suit initiated by the Audobon Society and the Mono Lake

Looking east toward Black Point, the retired volcano near which Mark Twain and Cal Higbie camped.

Committee at Lee Vining, has resulted in a court order which has temporarily prevented Los Angeles from diverting Rush Crek into its aqueduct. The level of the lake has risen and the land bridge to Negit Island is covered again by water. Not surprisingly, the birds have returned to Negit Island.

Mono Lake's water tastes bitter and is unfit to drink. However, it's useful for washing dirty clothing. Mark Twain wrote, "If you only dip the most hopelessly soiled garment into them [the waters] once or twice, and wring it out, it will be found as clean as if it had been through the ablest washerwomen's hands." But this is not entirely true today. The garment may have lost its dirty appearance but now will be filled with white chemicals only clean water can remove.

Because the water is so alkaline, it stings the eyes and wreaks holy terror for open cuts. Twain told of a dog he and Higbie had with raw places on him who made the mistake of venturing into Mono Lake for a swim. Twain wrote, "The alkali water nipped him in all the raw places simultaneously, and he struck out for the shore with considerable interest. He yelped and barked and howled as he went — and by the time he got to the shore there was no bark to him ... He finally struck out over the mountains, at a gait which we estimated at about two hundred and fifty miles an hour, and he is going yet. This was about nine years ago. We look for what is left of him along here every day." The story is probably a fabrication, but you get the picture: Mono Lake can be quite uncomfortable if you have an open cut.

Boating on Mono Lake, even today, can be very dangerous. Boats have capsized and unsuspecting persons have drowned when the still, mirror-like lake was quickly thrown into a raging sea by the Sierra's tempermental weather. Sam Clemens and Cal Higbie discovered for themselves how nasty the lake can be. In *Roughing It*, Mark Twain told of their excursion to Paoha Island and their near tragedy:

About seven o'clock one blistering hot morning — for it was now dead summertime — Higbie and I took the boat and started on a voyage of discovery to the two islands. We had often longed to do this, but had been deterred by the fear of storms; for they were frequent, and severe enough to capsize an ordinary rowboat like ours without great difficulty — and once capsized, death would ensue in spite of the bravest swimming, for that venomous water would eat a man's eyes out like fire, and burn him out inside, too,

The dark band are thousands of brine flies on the shoreline of Mono Lake. The flies are food for thousands of migrating birds. Paiute Indians gathered the pupae of the brine flies, dried them and made a kind of meal. Surprisingly, the food is supposed to have tasted quite good. *Photo Edie Williams.*

if he shipped a sea. It was called twelve miles, straight out to the islands — a long pull and a warm one — but the morning was so quiet and sunny, and the lake so smooth and glassy and dead, that we could not resist the temptation. So we filled two large tin canteens with water (since we were not acquainted with the locality of the springs said to exist on the large island), and started. Higbie's brawny muscles gave the boat good speed, but by the time we reached our destination we judged that we had pulled nearer fifteen miles than twelve.

We landed on the big island and went ashore. We tried the water in the canteens, now, and found that the sun had spoiled it; it was so brackish that we could not drink it; so we poured it out and began a search for the spring — for thirst augments fast as soon as it is apparent that one has no means at hand of quenching it. The island was a long, moderately big hill of ashes — nothing but gray ashes and pumice stone, in which we sunk to our knees at every step — and all around the top was a forbidding wall of scorched and blasted rocks. When we reached the top and got within the wall, we found simply a shallow, far-reaching basin, carpeted with ashes, and here and there a patch of fine sand. In places, picturesque jets of stream shot up out of the crevices, giving evidence that although this ancient crater had gone out of active business, there was still some fire left in its furnaces. Close to one of these jets of steam stood the only tree on the island — a small pine of most graceful shape and most faultless symmetry; its color was a brilliant green, for the steam drifted unceasingly through its branches and kept them always moist. It contrasted strangely enough, did this vigorous and beautiful outcast, with its dead and dismal surroundings. It was like a cheerful spirit in a mourning household.

We hunted for the spring everywhere, traversing the length of the island (two or three miles), and crossing it twice — climbing ash hills patiently, and then sliding down the other side in a sitting posture, plowing up smothering volumes of gray dust. But we found nothing but solitude, ashes and a heartbreaking silence. Finally we noticed that the wind had risen, and we forgot our thirst in a solicitude of greater importance; for the lake being quiet, we had not taken pains about securing the boat. We hurried back to a point overlooking our landing place, and then — but mere words

The sand tufa located at Navy Beach on the south shore of Mono Lake. *Photo Edie Williams.*

cannot describe our dismay — the boat was gone! The chances were that there was not another boat on the entire lake. The situation was not comfortable — in truth, to speak plainly, it was frightful. We were prisoners on a desolate island, in aggravating proximity to friends who were for the present helpless to aid us; and what was still more uncomfortable we had neither food nor water. But presently we sighted the boat. It was drifting along, leisurely, about fifty yards from shore, tossing in a foamy sea. It drifted, and continued to drift, but at the same safe distance from land, and we walked along abreast it and waited for fortune to favor us. At the end of an hour it approached a jutting cape, and Higbie ran ahead and posted himself on the utmost verge and prepared for the assault. If we failed there, there was no hope for us. It was driving gradually shoreward all the time, now; but whether it was driving fast enough to make the connection or not was the momentous question. When it got within thirty steps of Higbie I was so excited that I fancied I could hear my own heart beat. When, a little later, it dragged slowly along and seemed about to go by, only one little yard out of reach, it seemed as if my heart stood still; and when it was exactly abreast him and begun to widen away, and he still standing like a watching statue, I knew my heart did stop. But when he gave a great spring, the next instant, and lit fairly in the stern, I discharged a war whoop that woke the solitudes!

But it dulled my enthusiasm, presently, when he told me he had not been caring whether the boat came within jumping distance or not so that it passed within eight or ten yards of him, for he had made up his mind to shut his eyes and mouth and swim that trifling distance. Imbecile that I was, I had not thought of that. It was only a long swim that could be fatal.

The sea was running high and the storm increasing. It was growing late, too — three or four in the afternoon. Whether to venture toward the mainland or not was a question of some moment. But we were so distressed by thirst that we decided to try it, and so Higbie fell to work and I took the steering oar. When we had pulled a mile, laboriously, we were evidently in serious peril, for the storm had greatly augmented; the billows ran very high and were capped with foaming crests, the heavens were hung with black, and the wind blew with great fury. We would have

Here Mill Creek pours into Mono Lake. California Gulls feed on the brine shrimp and brine flies on the shoreline. Mark Twain and Cal Higbie camped near here in August, 1862. Mill Creek provided fresh water and there was plenty of drift wood along the creek for firewood. This place is walking distance from the Lee Vining Cemetery east of Mono Lake County Park on the northwestern shore.

gone back, now, but we did not dare to turn the boat around, because as soon as she got in the trough of the sea she would upset, of course. Our only hope lay in keeping her head-on to the seas. It was hard work to do this, she plunged so, and so beat and belabored the billows with her rising and falling bows. Now and then Higbie's oars would trip on the top of a wave, and the other one would snatch the boat half around in spite of my cumbersome steering apparatus. We were drenched by the sprays constantly, and the boat occasionally shipped water. By and by, powerful as my comrade was, his great exertions began to tell on him, and he was anxious that I should change places with him till he could rest a little. But I told him this was impossible; for if the steering oar were dropped a moment while we changed, the boat would slue around in the trough of the sea, capsize, and in less than five minutes we would have a hundred gallons of soapsuds in us and be eaten up so quickly that we could not even be present at our own inquest.

But things cannot last always. Just as darkness shut down we came booming into port, head-on. Higbie dropped his oars hurrah — I dropped mine to help — the sea gave the boat a twist, and over she went!

The agony that alkali water inflicts on bruises, chafes, and blistered hands is unspeakable, and nothing but greasing all over will modify it — but we ate, drank and slept well that night, notwithstanding.

Not only did Clemens consider the landscape dreary, he was not fond of Mono Lake's weather. He wrote:

There are only two seasons in the region round about Mono Lake — and these are, the breaking up of one winter and the beginning of the next. More than once (in Esmeralda) I have seen a perfectly blistering morning opening up with the thermometer at ninety degrees at eight o'clock, and seen the snow fall fourteen inches deep and that same identical thermometer go down to forty-four degrees under shelter, before nine o'clock at night. Under favorable circumstances it snows at least once in every single month in the year, in the little town of Mono [Monoville.] So uncertain is the climate in summer that a lady who goes visiting cannot hope

Aurora miners at work on the Prospectus Mine. *Nevada Historical Society.*

to be prepared for all emergencies unless she takes her fan under one arm and her snowshoes under the other. When they have a Fourth of July procession it generally snows on them and they do say that as a general thing when a man calls for a brandy toddy there, the barkeeper chops it off with a hatchet and wraps it up in a paper, like maple sugar. And it is further reported that the old soakers [drunks] haven't any teeth — wore them out eating gin cocktails and brandy punches. I do not endorse that statement — I simply give it for what it is worth — and it is worth — well, I should say, millions, to any man who can believe it without straining himself. But I do endorse the snow on the Fourth of July — because I know that to be true.

Roughing It

Mark Twain exaggerated the weather and the customs, of course. True, snowstorms can last until May but I have never known it to snow in July. Apparently, Clemens experienced a summer when it did snow on the fourth of July.

Nine Mile Ranch, once owned by Captain John Nye, located about 9 miles from Aurora on the graded dirt road to Sweetwater. Here Sam Clemens nursed John Nye for a week in early July, 1862.

CHAPTER EIGHT

Sam Clemens Leaves Aurora

By August 15, Clemens was back in Aurora and living with Dan Twing. Little is known of Dan Twing. Mark Twain did not mention him in *Roughing It*. The only recorded reference to Twing is in Clemens' August 15th letter to his sister, Pamela. This letter, published below, gives us an interesting glimpse of Clemens' last days in Aurora.

Esmeralda, Cal., Aug. 15, 1862

My dear Sister, — I mailed a letter to you and Ma this morning, but since then I have received yours to Orion and me. Therefore, I must answer right away, else I may leave town without doing it at all. What in thunder are pilot's wages to me? which question, I beg humbly to observe, is of a general *nature, and not discharged particularly at you. But it is singular, isn't it, that such a matter should interest Orion, when it is of no earthly consequence to me. I never have* once *thought of returning home to go on the river again, and I never expect to do any more piloting at any price. My livelihood must be made in this country — and if I have to wait longer than I expected, let it be so — I have no fear of failure. You know I have extravagant hopes, for Orion tells you everything which he ought to keep to himself — but it's his nature to do that sort of thing, and I let him alone. I did think for awhile of going home this fall — but when I found that that was and had been the cherished intention and the darling aspiration every year, of*

*these old care-worn Californians for twelve weary years — I felt
a little uncomfortable, but I stole a march on Disappointment and
said I would not go home this fall. I will spend the winter in San
Francisco, if possible. Do not tell any one that I had any idea of
piloting again at present — for it is all a mistake. This country
suits me, and — it shall suit me, whether or no ...*

*Dan Twing and I and Dan's dog, "Cabin" together — and will
continue to do so for awhile — until I leave for —*

*The mansion is 10x12, with a "domestic" roof. Yesterday it
rained — the first shower for five months. "Domestic," it appears
to me, is not water-proof. We went outside to keep from getting
wet. Dan makes the bed when it is his turn to do it — and when
it is my turn, I don't you know. The dog is not a good hunter,
and he isn't worth shucks to watch — but he scratches up the dirt
floor of the cabin, and catches flies, and makes himself generally
useful in the way of washing dishes. Dan gets up first in the
morning and makes a fire — and I get up last and sit by it, while
he cooks breakfast. We have a cold lunch at noon, and I cook
supper — very much against my will. However, one must have
one good meal a day, and if I were to live on Dan's abominable
cookery, I should lose my appetite, you know. Dan attended Dr.
Corpenning's funeral yesterday, and he felt as though he ought
to wear a white shirt — and we had a jolly good time finding such
an article. We turned over all our traps, and he found one at last
— but I shall always think it was suffering from yellow fever. He
also found an old black coat, greasy, and wrinkled to that degree
that it appeared to have been quilted at some time or other. In
this gorgeous costume he attended the funeral. And when he
returned, his own dog drove him away from the cabin, not
recognizing him. This is true.*

*You would not like to live in a country where flour was $40
a barrel? Very well, then, I suppose you would not like to live here,
where flour was $100 a barrel when I first came here. And shortly
afterwards, it couldn't be had at any price — and for a month
the people lived on barley, beans and beef — and nothing beside.
Oh, no — we didn't luxuriate then! Perhaps not. But we said wise
and severe things about the vanity and wickedness of high living.
We preached our doctrine and practised it. Which course I
respectfully recommend to clergymen of St. Louis.*

Where is Beck Jolly? and [Horace] Bixby?
Your Brother,
    Sam.

That Clemens had apparently considered going back to river piloting is no surprise considering his hard times at Aurora. Even though he has extravagant hopes and things haven't gone as expected, for all his complaining to Orion, he tells Pamela that the country suits him whether he succeeds or not. Clemens was not afraid of failure. His lack of fear freed him to be a risk taker and adventurous. This character trait would help him immeasurably during his long career.

About eleven days after this letter, August 26, Clemens left Aurora again for two weeks. When he returned to Aurora, he wrote Billy Claggett, September 9, "For more than two weeks I have been slashing around in the White Mountain District, partly for pleasure and partly for other reasons. And old Van Horn was in the party ... We had rare good times out there fishing for trout and hunting. I mean to go out there again before long." As mentioned earlier, Van Horn was a miner from Lee Vining affiliated with Whiteman and his search for the lost cement gold mine. Whether Clemens was with Van Horn and Higbie in search of the lost cement gold mine is not certain. This trip appears to have been more for pleasure.

The White Mountains are a light colored mountain range running north to south. They are about twenty miles east of the Sierra Nevada and run parallel to the Sierra. The highest peak in the range, White Mountain Peak, is 14,246 feet, nearly as high as Mt. Whitney. Between the White Mountains and the Sierra range is a valley. The northern part are highlands of green grasslands where glassy, clear mountain streams wind their way to the Owens River. The southern portion is known as Owens Valley, a narrow strip of desert land where the Paiutes lived. The Owens River winds its way through the Owens Valley to Owens Lake, once large and blue, today a white alkali sump caused by the diversion of the Owens River into the Los Angeles aqueduct.

Long Valley, in the high country, was once a beautiful green valley where the Owens River wound through unhindered. In the 1940's a dam was built at the southern end of Long Valley to contain the river and formed Crowley Lake which covers part of Long Valley today.

Sam Clemens probably visited Long Valley on his last hiking trip. High in the mountains it would have been cool and the trout fishing would have been good on the Owens River. The distance is about 60 miles from Aurora. Clemens likely traveled along the Aurora to Owens River Road which led south from Aurora across the Mono Basin east of Mono Lake to the mountains. He probably crossed Adobe Meadows southeast of Mono Lake and followed the wagon road into the mountains. He would have then followed Dexter Creek up Wild Cow Canyon east of Bald Mountain. At the head of Wild Cow Canyon he could look down and see Long Valley, green and alluring, below the towering Sierra Nevada. He followed McLaughlin Creek Canyon down to the Owens River and to Long Valley. This is inspiring country, cool in the mountains and there are plenty of springs and streams for water.

Returning to Aurora around September 9, Clemens received word from William Barstow that he should begin reporting for the *Enterprise* in October. He would have about a month to learn the ropes. In November, Dan De Quille, the reporter Clemens was to replace, would be leaving for the East to visit his family.

Broke and somewhat discouraged because he had failed to strike it rich, Sam Clemens, with a bed roll strapped across his back, left Aurora for Virginia City on foot. He followed the wagon road past Nine Mile Ranch and along the East Walker River north. He was probably glad to rid himself of the hard times he had experienced at Aurora.

But Clemens' hard won knowledge of mining and the miners' life would prove an invaluable stepping stone to his reporting career at Virginia City. At Aurora, Clemens became a full fledged silver miner. He learned to distinguish rich gold and silver bearing ore from poor. He learned to blast tunnels and sink shafts, to mill and assay. And, ne learned to speak the miner's peculiar language of "feet", "ledges," "drifts," "stopes," and "buttons." Most importantly, by being a miner himself, Clemens was able to understand the miner's dreams and failures and the emotional ups and downs a silver miner goes through daily. All he learned at Aurora would be useful as Clemens took up his new job as reporter for the *Territorial Enterprise*, at Virginia City, Nevada, the richest mining town in the West.

Editor's Note: To continue this series of books on Mark Twain's life in the West, read, *MARK TWAIN: His Life In Virginia City, Nevada,* by the author. You may order this autographed book directly from this publisher by using the order form on the last page.

The road Sam Clemens walked down on his way to Virginia City from Aurora. This site is near Nine Mile Ranch.

CHRONOLOGY

July 26, 1861 - Sam Clemens, twenty-five years old, leaves St. Joseph, Missouri by Overland stage with his older brother, Orion, recently appointed Secretary of Nevada Territory.

August 14 - Sam and Orion arrive in Carson City and take up residence at Bridget O'Flannagans boarding house. The trouble begins.

Late August - Sam makes his first trip to Lake Tahoe, then called Lake Bigler, with John Kinney.

Early September - Makes his second trip to Lake Tahoe with Tom Nye. Stays three weeks and claims 300 acres of timber. "House" burns down and returns to Carson City.

October - Makes his first trip to Aurora, 130 miles south of Carson City, to inspect the silver mines. Horatio Phillips gives Sam 50 feet in the Black Warrior claim.

Mid-October - Returns to Carson City.

October 26 - Writes the first of several correspondent letters for the St. Louis, *Gate City*. These letters form the basis for parts of *Roughing It*.

November 30 - Turns twenty-six.

December 8-16 - Some time during this week, Sam and three friends leave Carson City for Unionville, Humboldt Mining District, 200 miles northeast of Carson City.

December 23-31 - Sam and his partners arrive in Unionville after a weary and cold journey.

January 1-14 - Sam and his partners build a temporary rock and shrub shelter and begin prospecting the hills for silver ledges. Sam becomes discouraged.

Mid-January, 1862 - Sam returns to Carson City.

Early April - Clemens journeys on horseback to Aurora, 130 miles south of Carson City, in hopes of striking it rich in the silver mines.

April 13 - Writes his first letter from Aurora to Orion in Carson City.

April 28 - Sam and partner Horatio Phillips, working on their Dashaway claim.

May - Some time during this month, Sam begins writing humorous letters about a hard luck miner's life in the mining camps. He signs the letters "Josh" and mails them to the *Territorial Enterprise* at Virginia City. The letters are published to Clemens' surprise.

May 11 - Sam's mining dealings intensify. Part owner of several claims, the Black Warrior, the Dashaway, the Monitor and the Flyaway.

May 17 - Writes Orion that the Monitor claim has been jumped. Sam seeks legal counsel.

June 2 - Monitor suit is settled in court; Sam and Horatio essentially win. Sam, Horatio and Bob Howland are part owners in the Annipolitan, a promising claim located next to the Wide West, a rich gold mine.

June 22 - Sam and Horatio feverishly work the Annipolitan and Flyaway claims.

June 25 - In need of money, Clemens considers writing correspondent letters for some newspaper. Asks Orion to help him get work for the Sacramento *Union*.

July 9 - About this time, Clemens nurses Captain Nye at Nine Mile Ranch near Aurora. First mentions Cal Higbie, to whom Twain dedicated *Roughing It*. Also refers to Whiteman's lost cement gold mine.

July 23 - Apparently, Clemens and Horatio Phillips have a falling out. Clemens is deeply in debt; none of his mines have paid off.

July 30 - Notifies Orion that he has been offered a reporting post by the *Territorial Enterprise*.

August 7 - Writes Orion that he will accept the reporting position. About this time takes a walking trip. Goes fishing at Trumboll Lake for a week and visits Mono Lake for the first time.

August 15 - Living with Dan Twing in a cabin. Broke, may have gone to work at a stamp mill in order to earn money.

August 26 - Takes a 60-70 mile hike to the White Mountain District, probably in search of new prospects. May have visited Long Valley, today's Crowley Lake near Mammoth Lakes, California.

September 9 - Writes his last letter from Aurora to Billy Claggett.

Early-October, 1862 - Broke and discouraged, Clemens leaves Aurora by foot on a 130 mile journey to Virginia City. There he begins a two year reporting career and adopts Mark Twain as his pen name.

ACKNOWLEDGEMENTS

As always, I thank my wife, Edie, for her love, encouragement, support and prayers. My wife has given unselfishly of herself during the ups and downs of this author's career. Edie also read the manuscript, caught misspellings and other errors.

I thank the Mark Twain Project, University of Califoroa, Berkeley, for making available Mark Twain's letters. The staff supplied the author with copies of the letters and reproduced some photographs which appear in this book. I also thank the Mark Twain project for permission to publish portions of Mark Twain's letters.

Edmund Berkeley, Jr., Curator of Manuscripts at the University of Virginia Library, promptly supplied a photograph of Mark Twain's June 22, 1862 letter. I also thank Mr. Berkeley for permission to publish this letter.

Thanks again to Phil Earl, Nevada Historical Society, for aid in locating photographs of Aurora.

My father, George Williams, Jr., located a camera the author was sorely in need of. Thank you.

Last, but always first, I thank you Lord, Jesus Christ, for your help with this book, for my wife and children, for my work and for the good life you have given me here on your earth.

BIBLIOGRAPHY

The following is a partial bibliography students and scholars may find useful.

Unpublished sources:

The Mark Twain Papers. Mark Twain Project, University of California, Berkeley

Newspapers:

Aurora Borealis
Bodie Evening Miner
Bridgeport-Chronicle Union
Gold Hill News
Territorial Enterprise

Books:

Benson, Ivan: *Mark Twain's Western Years,* Russell and Russell, 1938.

Brand, Edgar Marquis: *The Literary Apprenticeship of Mark Twain,* University of Illinois Press, 1958.

DeVoto, Bernard: *Mark Twain's America,* Houghton Mifflin Company, 1932.

Gaines, David: *Mono Lake Guidebook,* Mono Lake Committee/Kutsavi Books, 1981.

Long, E. Hudson: *Mark Twain Handbook,* Hendricks House, 1957.

Mack, Effid Mona: *Mark Twain In Nevada,* Charles Scribner's Sons, 1947.

Paine, Albert Bigelow: *Mark Twain: A Biography,* Harper and Bros., 1912. Mark Twain's Letters, Vol. 1, Harper and Bros., 1917.

Rogers, Franklin: *The Pattern For Mark Twain's Roughing It,* University of California Press, 1961

Twain, Mark: *The Autobiography of Mark Twain,* Edited by charles Neider, Harper and Row, 1959; *Roughing It; The Innocents Abroad.*

Wasson, Joseph: *Bodie and Esmeralda,* Spaulding, Barto and Co., San Francisco, 1878.

Wedertz, Frank S.: *Bodie 1859-1900,* Chalfant Press, 1969. *Mono Diggings*, Chalfant Press, 1978.

Williams, George J., III: *The Guide To Bodie and Eastern Sierra Historic Sites,* Tree By The River Publishing, 1981. *Rosa May, The Search For a Mining Camp Legend,* Tree By The River Publishing, 1980.

Records:

Esmeralda Mining District Records at Mono County Clerk's Office, Bridgeport, California.

Order these great books by mail today
Autographed and inscribed by George Williams III

NEW! In the Last of the Wild West. The true story of the author's attempt to expose the murders of prostitutes and corruption in Virginia City, Storey County, Nevada, home of the largest legal brothel in the United States. 272 pages. AUTOGRAPHED. $12.95 quality paperback; $24.95 hard cover.

ROSA MAY: THE SEARCH FOR A MINING CAMP LEGEND Virginia city, Carson City and Bodie, California were towns Rosa May worked as a prostitute and madam 1873-1912. Read her remarkable true story based on 3 1/2 years of research. Praised by the *Los Angeles Times* and *Las Vegas Review Journal*. Includes 30 rare photos, 26 personal letters. 240 pages. AUTOGRAPHED. $10.95 quality paperback; hard cover, $16.95. Soon to be a television movie.

THE REDLIGHT LADIES OF VIRGINIA CITY, NEVADA Virginia City was the richest mining camp in the American West. The silver from its mines built San Francisco and helped the Union win the Civil War. From 1860-95, Virginia City had three of the largest redlight districts in America. Here women from around the world worked the world's oldest profession. Author Williams tells the stories of the strange lives of the redlight girls, their legends and violent deaths. Based on newspaper accounts, county records and U.S. Census information. Perhaps the best and most informative book on prostitution in the old West. Plenty of historic photos, illustrations, map and letters. 48 pages. AUTOGRAPHED. $5.95 quality paperback; hard cover, $10.95.

HOT SPRINGS OF THE EASTERN SIERRA Here are more than 40 natural hot spring pools author George Williams III has located from the Owens Valley, through the Eastern Sierra recreation corridor to Gerlach, Nevada. George has tracked down every hot spring worth "soaking" in. Included are many secret springs only known to locals. George gives easy to follow road directions, and his "2 cents" about each spring are informative and entertaining. Maps by the author help you find these secret springs easily. 72 pages. AUTOGRAPHED. $6.95 quality paperback; hard cover, $12.95.

THE GUIDE TO BODIE AND EASTERN SIERRA HISTORIC SITES True story of the rise and fall of Bodie, California's most famous mining camp, today a ghost town, National Historic Site and California State Park. Known as the toughest gold mining town in the West where millions were made in a few years, murders were a daily occurrence. Has a beautiful full color cover with 100 photos on an 8 1/2 X 11 format. 88 pages. AUTOGRAPHED. $10.95 quality paperback; hard cover, $16.95.

THE MURDERS AT CONVICT LAKE True story of the infamous 1871 Nevada State Penitentiary break in which 29 outlaws escaped and fled more than 250 miles into Mono and Inyo counties, California. They vowed to kill anyone who got in their way. In a terrible shootout at Monte Diablo, today known as Convict Lake just south of Mammoth Lakes ski resort, the convicts killed two men. They fled to nearby Bishop where they were captured and hanged. Includes 18 rare photographs and pen and ink drawings by Dave Comstock. 32 pages. AUTOGRAPHED. $4.95 quality paperback; hard cover, $12.95.

MARK TWAIN: HIS ADVENTURES AT AURORA AND MONO LAKE When Sam Clemens arrived in Nevada in 1861, he wanted to get rich quick. He tried silver mining at Aurora, Nevada near Mono Lake not far from Yosemite National Park. Clemens didn't strike it rich but his hard luck mining days led to his literary career. 32 rare photos, mining deeds and maps to places where Clemens lived, wrote and camped. 100 pages. AUTOGRAPHED. $6.95 quality paperback; hard cover, $12.95.

NEW! MARK TWAIN: HIS LIFE IN VIRGINIA CITY, NEVADA While reporting for the *Territorial Enterprise* in Virginia City, 1862-64, Sam Clemens adopted his well known pen name, Mark Twain. Here is the lively account of Mark Twain's early writing days in the most exciting town in the West. Over 60 rare photos and maps to places Twain lived and wrote. 208 pages. AUTOGRAPHED. $10.95 paperback; hard cover, $24.95.

Mark Twain: Jackass Hill and the Jumping Frog by George Williams III. The true story of Twain's discovery of "The Celebrated Jumping Frog of Calaveras County," the publication of which launched his international career. After getting run out of Virginia City, Twain settled in San Francisco in May, 1864. He went to work as a common reporter for the San Francisco *Call*. After five frustrating months, Twain quit the *Call* and began hanging around with Bret Harte, then editor of the popular *Golden Era*, a West Coast magazine. When Twain posted bail for a friend and the friend skipped town, Twain followed and headed for Jackass Hill in the foothills of the Sierra Nevada near Sonora. There Twain lived with his prospector friend Jim Gillis in a one room log cabin on Jackass Hill. After a discouraging prospecting trip, in a saloon at Angel's Camp, Twain was told the Jumping Frog story by a bartender. Twain's version, published eleven months later, became an international hit. "The Celebrated Jumping Frog of Calaveras County," is included in this book.
72 pages, index, bibliography, 35 historic photographs, guide maps for travelers. AUTOGRAPHED. Quality paper $6.95; hard cover $12.95

New for Spring 1992! On the Road with Mark Twain in California and Nevada Here is a handy, easy to read guide to Mark Twain's haunts in California and Nevada 1861-68. Has road directions to historic sites, guide maps and lots of photographs of Twain, the historic sites and Twain's friends. Gives brief run-downs of each place and tells what Twain was doing while there. A must-have book for any Twain fan who would like to follow his trail in the far West. 150 pages, many photos, road maps, index. $12.95 quality paper; $24.95 hard cover.